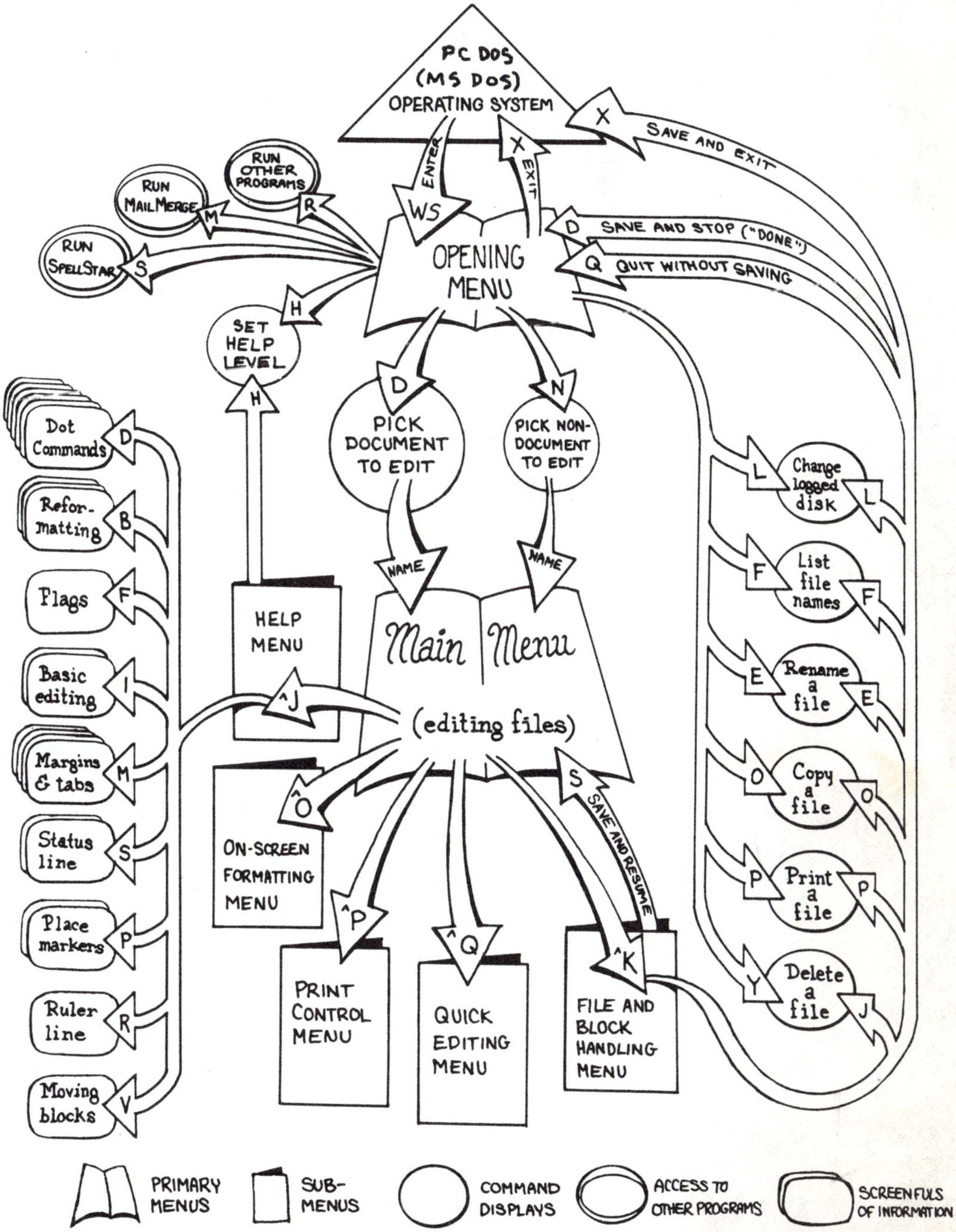
PC DOS
(MS DOS)
OPERATING SYSTEM
ENTER
WS
EXIT
X
X
SAVE AND EXIT
RUN OTHER PROGRAMS
R
RUN MAILMERGE
M
RUN SPELLSTAR
S
D
SAVE AND STOP ("DONE")
Q
QUIT WITHOUT SAVING
OPENING MENU
H
SET HELP LEVEL
H
D
PICK DOCUMENT TO EDIT
N
PICK NON-DOCUMENT TO EDIT
NAME
NAME
Main Menu
(editing files)
HELP MENU
^J
^O
ON-SCREEN FORMATTING MENU
^P
PRINT CONTROL MENU
^Q
QUICK EDITING MENU
S
SAVE AND RESUME
^K
FILE AND BLOCK HANDLING MENU
Dot Commands
D
Refor-matting
B
Flags
F
Basic editing
I
Margins & tabs
M
Status line
S
Place markers
P
Ruler line
R
Moving blocks
V
L
Change logged disk
L
F
List file names
F
E
Rename a file
E
O
Copy a file
O
P
Print a file
P
Y
Delete a file
J
PRIMARY MENUS
SUB-MENUS
COMMAND DISPLAYS
ACCESS TO OTHER PROGRAMS
SCREENFULS OF INFORMATION

MASTERING WORDSTAR ON THE IBM PC

MASTERING WORDSTAR™ ON THE IBM® PC

ARTHUR NAIMAN

A version of
Introduction to WordStar
adapted by MEG HOLMBERG

FIRST
EDITION

SYBEX®

BERKELEY • PARIS • DÜSSELDORF • LONDON

Cover Art by Kurt Fink
Technical Illustrations by Jeanne E. Tennant

WordStar, MailMerge, SpellStar, DataStar, SuperSort, TelMerge, StarIndex, ReportStar, CalcStar, and CorrectStar are trademarks of MicroPro International.
IBM is a registered trademark of International Business Machines Corporation.

Library of Congress Card Number: 85-63781
ISBN 0-89588-250-7
Printed by Haddon Craftsmen
Manufactured in the United States of America
10 9 8 7 6 5 4 3 2

This book is dedicated to
Ron Lichty
who deserves to have a book dedicated to him
and to
Isaac Asimov
whose popular science writing sets the standard
for clarity and intelligent organization.

Table of Contents

5 *The Control-Character Menus*

6 *Moving and Deleting Blocks of Text*

7 *Global Searches and Substitutions*

8 *File Handling*

Acknowledgments

I want to thank Rudolph Langer, whose taste in restaurants is almost as good as his taste in authors; Janet Rampa, who made many useful suggestions; Gar Smith, who did a terrific job in no time at all; Tony Pietsch, who was—as always—a big help; Dr. Jerome Z. Litt, who made an incisive correction; Connie Gatto, without whom everything would fall apart; and Ira Rosenberg, Gloria Zarifa, Cheryl Nichols, Vic Fischer, Rita Gibian and Albert Naiman, whose support has been invaluable.

David Kolodney did a very intelligent job of editing (and of knowing when not to edit, which is a much rarer skill). Other people who have contributed to the book in its various incarnations are Valerie Brewster, Jim Compton, Jannie Dresser, Jeremy Elliott, Elaine Foster, Barbara Gordon, Bonnie Gruen, Doug Hergert, Mike Howard, Ingrid Owen, Valerie Robbins, Bret Rohmer, Donna Scanlon, Sarah Seaver, Olivia Shinomoto, Mati Sikk, j. trujillo smith, Jeanne E. Tennant, Hilda van Genderen, Galdys Varon, Cheryl Wilcox Vega, Eileen Walsh, and Judy Wohlfrom.

Arthur Naiman

Introduction

Since early 1982, *Introduction to WordStar* has provided a well-organized, clearly written guide to MicroPro's popular word processing program. In the third edition of that book, an appendix was added for users of the program on the IBM Personal Computer, the Compaq and other MS DOS machines. By now, WordStar is used more frequently on the PC and compatibles than on the CP/M machines it was originally written for. So an edition specifically tailored for that audience seemed in order, and here it is.

If you're already using WordStar, *Mastering WordStar on the IBM PC* will clarify the workings of features you have only a foggy comprehension of, or that you don't even know exist. (It's a rare WordStar owner who really understands what the program can do.)

If you've just bought WordStar for your PC, this book will teach you how it works more quickly and easily than MicroPro's manuals (which are better used for reference than as primers). If you're considering buying WordStar, you'll get an excellent sense of the program's capabilities and of whether you can use it to accomplish what you want.

If you just want a good idea of what word processing programs do, this book will give you one, using WordStar as an example. (There aren't many features that WordStar doesn't have.)

One thing *Mastering WordStar on the IBM PC* won't do is replace MicroPro's manuals. Its aim is to introduce subjects, not to exhaustively describe them.

The book is written as if you're running the program while you read it, which is definitely what you should do if you own WordStar. But my approach also works well if you don't. Since I show what appears on the screen at every turn, and discuss exactly what happens as the result of every command, reading *Mastering WordStar on the IBM PC* gives you as close a sense of what WordStar feels like as anything short of actually using the program.

When I talk about features, or how the menus look, I'm referring to versions 3.3 and 3.31. The first version of WordStar for the PC was 3.2, and when things work differently in that version, I make note of it. You should also be aware that some 3.2 menus are worded and arranged slightly differently than the ones shown in this book.

WordStar commands and word processing terms and concepts are boldfaced where they're first discussed (which is usually—but not always—the first time they're mentioned). This book is organized as logically as possible, and tries to present information in the most useful order. But the structure of WordStar itself often makes this difficult. Unrelated commands are sometimes grouped together on a menu, and a command on one menu can play an important role on another.

To take care of the occasional times when a term or concept is mentioned before it's been properly introduced, I've provided a very detailed index. The boldfaced page number indicates where the word is boldfaced in the book, and therefore where it's most fully explained. The other page numbers show how the term or command is used in various contexts. Because the index is so complete, *Mastering WordStar on the IBM PC* can be used as a reference as well as for step-by-step training.

Chapter 1 is a general introduction to word processing for readers who are unfamiliar with what word processing is. Chapter 2 discusses WordStar's particular strengths as a word processing program. Chapter 3 gives you a taste of WordStar by walking you through the writing of a somewhat whimsical business letter.

Chapters 4 through 8 explain how to edit with WordStar, and Chapters 9 through 11 explain how to format and print out. Chapter 12 covers the optional MailMerge program, with which you can generate form letters and other repetitive documents. Chapter 13 covers MicroPro's optional spelling checker, SpellStar.

Appendix A is a quick reference summary of all the WordStar commands, grouped by what they do and laid out graphically. Appendix B does the same for MailMerge and Appendix C for SpellStar. Appendix D is a map of WordStar. It shows the overall organization of the program and how the various menus and command displays connect with each other. (This map also serves as the frontispiece for the book.)

If you're using an older version of WordStar (before 3.3), you'll also want to look at Appendix E, "A Special Note for Earlier Versions of WordStar."

1 Word Processing: What It Is and What It Can Do for You

BASICALLY, a **word processor** does what a typewriter does, only better. The main difference between the two is that on a word processor, what you write is stored as electronic (or magnetic) impulses, instead of as marks on paper. Word processors can do this because they're computers that have been programmed to let you type in text, edit it, and have it printed out.

All word processors are computers; **dedicated word processors** are just computers that can't do anything *but* word processing. When I refer to a word processor in this book, all I mean is a computer that's running a word processing program, regardless of whether that computer was called a "word processor" when it was sold. In fact, for the purposes of this book, I use the terms "word processor" and "computer" pretty much interchangeably.

You type on a word processor just as you do on a typewriter, but instead of the text appearing on a piece of paper, you see it on a screen—a **CRT** or **cathode ray tube** similar to the one on your television set (but without a tuner to pick up stations). The text shows up on paper only when you order a **printout** (also called a **hard copy**).

Revising without Retyping

The main advantage of this is that you can change what you've written as many times as you like, without having to retype any part you leave unchanged.

For example, let's say that when I originally wrote this chapter, this paragraph wasn't included. On rereading, I realized I wanted to add something at this point. All I had to do was move to the beginning of the next paragraph (the one that starts "Or consider . . . "), push a key, and start writing. A new paragraph was inserted here; the next paragraph (and everything that follows it) was pushed down.

Or consider how easy it was for me to remove the paragraph after this one (the one that isn't there now—the digression about terraforming on Ganymede). All I had to do was move to the start of it and hit a key for each line I wanted to kill. The text below moved up to fill the gap. (I could also have deleted the whole paragraph in one fell swoop, with a different command.)

It doesn't matter when, or how often, you make a printout of the text. You can go through twenty drafts without ever putting one on paper. Or you can make dozens of printouts. You can start changing a printout the instant it's finished, just as if you'd never put a word on paper, and have a new draft printed out as soon as you're done. This gives you the freedom to make whatever changes are necessary, without having to worry about all the retyping that such changes would normally involve.

A word processor also lets you:

- change a word (or an entire phrase) everywhere it occurs in a manuscript, in a matter of seconds;
- move whole sections of text around from one place to another (and then move them back again if you want);
- find the next (or last) occurrence of any word or phrase; and
- store blocks of text and print them out in various combinations.

Special Print Effects

When you go to print out your text, you have available several effects you can't get (or can't get easily) with a typewriter. Some examples are boldface, automatically centered lines, justified (i.e., straight) right margins, automatic page numbering, automatically indented blocks of text, and automatic paging (that is, the word processor knows to move the printout to the next page when the page it's on gets full).

For certain kinds of projects, word processors are virtually indispensable—as, for example, when you need to send the same (or a similar) letter to a lot of different people. You type the basic letter only once, and then just change the name (and whatever else you want) on subsequent letters. If you have a program like MailMerge, the computer will even do these substitutions for you. The finished product looks like it's been individually typed, and in fact it has been—but by the word processor, not by you.

How Word Processors Work

That's what word processors can do; now I'll explain how they do it. The chart below shows the basic components that make up a word processor.

Any—or all—of these components can be combined in the same box (although in word processing applications, the printer is usually separate). Each kind of component has the same functions from one computer system to the next, regardless of whether they're packaged together or not. The IBM PC puts the storage unit and the computer into the same box.

The equipment that makes up a computer system is called **hardware.** The instructions that tell the hardware what to do are called **software** or **programs**.

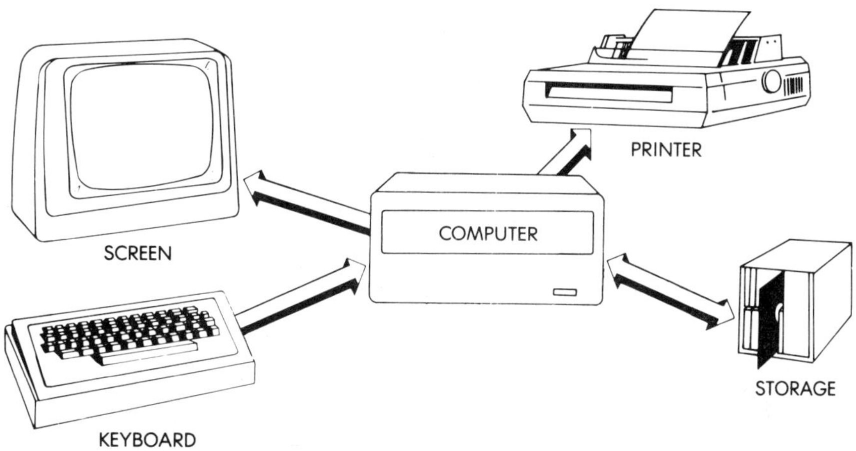

Basic Components of a Word Processor

The arrows in the chart show the *direction of information flow.* Information flows only from the keyboard to the computer, never from the computer to the keyboard. And information flows only *to* the screen, never from it (unless you have a light pen or touch-sensitive screen, neither of which are very useful on a word processor).

Control Characters

The keyboard on a PC works much the same as one on a typewriter, with a few major differences. One difference is the **control key.** The control key is similar to the shift key in one respect: they both change the effect of other keys.

For example, if you hit the *a* key while holding the shift key down, you get *A* instead of *a*. On the letter keys, the shift key always gives you a capital letter. On number keys, it gives you a symbol—&, $, (, or). On symbol keys, it gives you another symbol—: for ;, or ? for /.

Everything the shift key produces shows up on the screen, and subsequently on paper. Not so for the control key. If you hold it down while hitting another key, you get a **control character.** Control characters generally don't appear on the screen or on paper. Instead, they *do* things. Control-D, for example, might move the cursor one space to the right.

It becomes bothersome always to have to write "control-" whenever you want to refer to a control character, so a standard convention has been adopted. The ^ symbol, immediately followed by a

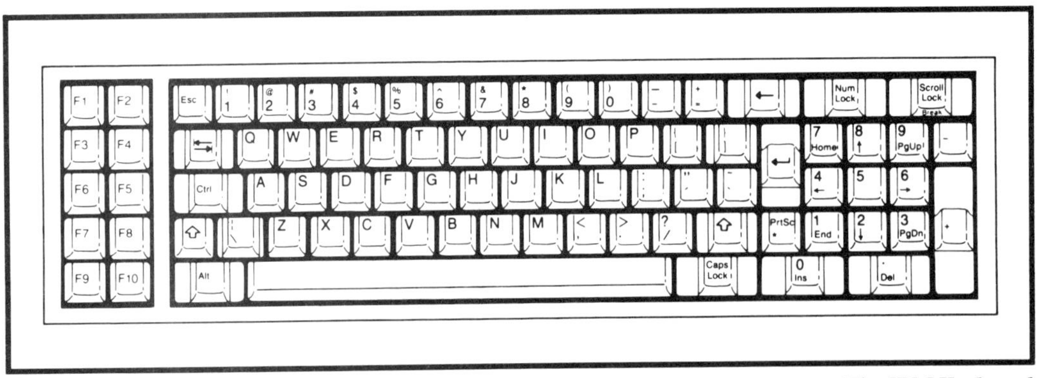

The IBM Keyboard

letter (^A, ^S, etc.), means "hold down the control key while hitting that letter." (In this book, that's all ^ will mean, since WordStar doesn't use the ^ key.)

Control characters are written in caps to make them easier to pick out of the text, but it doesn't matter whether you also hold down the shift key, as well as the control key, while hitting the letter: ^X and ^x have the same effect.

The Cursor

On a typewriter, you know where you are by the position of the ribbon slot (the place where the letters hit the paper). But on a word processor, the ribbon slot is on the printer, and the text is on the screen. So you need some sort of marker to tell you where you are in the text. This marker is called the **cursor.** On the IBM PC, it's a flashing underline mark.

As you type, the cursor moves along. Each new letter appears on the space where the cursor was, and the cursor then moves to the next space to the right. (The cursor also indicates the place where text is going to be deleted or changed.)

Memory and Storage

When text appears on a word processor's screen, it's simultaneously stored in the computer's **memory** (actually, it's stored in the memory first, and then displayed on the screen, but both happen virtually simultaneously). The portion of memory you write your text in is called **RAM** (for "random access memory"), **read/write memory,** or **R/W memory**.

Since a computer's memory goes blank when you turn the computer off, you must store what you want to keep on **floppy disks** (also called **diskettes** or **floppies**).

Floppies are one of several kinds of **storage media.** *Storage*—implying a certain amount of permanence—is distinguished from *memory*—which in computers (unlike elephants) is ephemeral.

Floppies are the word processor's equivalent of filing cabinet drawers. Each will hold several dozen **files.** A file is any piece of text that you give a name. It can be thousands of words long or just one word long. You can split long files in two and combine short files into one. You decide what makes up a file by giving a chunk of text a distinct name.

A floppy looks sort of like a 45-rpm record in its jacket and is made of essentially the same stuff as recording tape. Floppies are enclosed in square jackets, which are about 1/16" thick and measure either 8" or 5¼" on each side (even smaller ones have been introduced). The IBM PC uses 5¼" mini-diskettes.

Information is **written** onto floppies, and **read** off of them, by devices called **disk drives.** This is done by a **read/write head,** which is mounted at the end of a short arm that moves back and forth over the disks while they spin around at high speed.

Files can also be stored on something called a **hard disk.** (The IBM PC model XT contains a hard disk inside its central unit.) For the purposes of this book, I ignore the distinction between hard and floppy disks and refer to floppies simply as **disks.**

The capacity of different floppies varies greatly, depending not only on their size but also on whether information is written on both sides **(double-sided)** or just one side **(single-sided)**, and on how densely the information is recorded **(single-density** or **double-density)**.

In WordStar, the maximum length of a file depends on the capacity of the disk. Depending on your system, that can be as many as a million words (on systems that have a hard disk).

Text Files and Programs

There are two basic kinds of files: data files and programs. In the case of word processing, the data in a **data file** is text, and thus it's called a **text file.**

A **program** is made up of instructions. Programs tell computers how to do things. As the user of a word processor, you will not be making up your own programs (although, of course, you can also do programming on the side). You'll be using a **word processing program** called WordStar. WordStar is a set of instructions that tells your computer how to do word processing. With it, you can create, edit, and print out your own text files.

Word processing programs are made up of two parts—the **editor** (also called the **text editor**), which lets you insert, delete, and change text; and the **formatter,** which lets you control how that text appears on paper (and, in the case of WordStar, how it appears on the screen).

Sometimes the phrase "word processor" is used to refer to a word processing program itself, rather than the whole computer system on which the program runs. Context always makes it clear which is being talked about.

Loading is the name for transferring a file from disk to memory. When a file is loaded, a copy of it is made and put in the computer's memory. (The original copy on the disk is unaffected.)

Saving is the name for transferring a file from memory to disk. A copy of the file in the computer's memory is put on the disk. The file in memory remains unchanged (unless you change it or turn the computer off, that is).

Both programs and data files are stored on disks, and both can be loaded or saved. But, generally, you don't save programs, because you don't change them when they're in memory. You simply load them into memory so that you can use them.

The disk drive that a file will be loaded from or saved to (if you don't specify another) is called the **logged drive** (usually drive A). The disk in that drive is called the **logged disk.** WordStar allows you to change the logged drive.

The Operating System

In order for your word processor to be able to load any file, you will first have to **boot** it—that is, load a very basic program, called an **operating system,** that tells the computer how to load other programs. In the case of the IBM PC, this program is called PC-DOS if you're using the IBM PC, MS-DOS if you're using a PC compatible. (PC-DOS is just another name for MS-DOS). The word "boot" comes from the idea that the computer system pulls itself up by its own bootstraps. Refer to your system's manual if you don't know how to boot it.

That's enough about word processing in general. The next chapter talks about the virtues and capabilities of the WordStar word processing program in particular.

2 The WordStar Word Processing Program: What's Good about It

WORDSTAR has just about every bell and whistle you get with any other word processing system, and then some. The most impressive thing about it is all the different things it can do. This is what we mean when we say that WordStar is a very *powerful* editor.

On-Screen Formatting

Many of the features now found on most powerful word processing programs were introduced first in WordStar. One is **on-screen formatting**, which means you see line breaks, page breaks, paragraphs, centering, margins (top, bottom and side), etc. on the screen and can change them before printing out.

Word Wrap

Another useful feature is **word wrap**. Word wrap means that you don't have to put the equivalent of a carriage return (the key labeled ↵) at the end of each line. When a word runs over the end of a line, WordStar automatically moves the *whole* word down to the next line. You just keep typing. The ↵ key is used only when you want to force a line break, as at the end of a paragraph, or to create a blank line.

Another useful feature is that text is kept on the disk and automatically moved back and forth between the computer's memory and the disk as needed. Because of that, the maximum size of a file (a piece of text you're working on) is limited only by the amount of space on the disk. This means that a file can be much longer than it could if it were limited to the size of your PC's RAM (the amount of workspace your computer provides you).

Because almost all of a WordStar file is on the disk and only a little bit of it is in RAM, you can use one part of RAM to print out a file while using another part of RAM to work on another file.

Other Programs

Another advantage of WordStar is the large number of **ancillary programs** that work with it. There are programs available to:

- proof text (i.e., catch typos and spelling errors)
- prepare indexes
- merge mailing lists or pieces of "boilerplate" into customized form letters that appear to be individually typed
- sort information into alphabetical (or other kinds of) order

On-Screen Help

MicroPro is proud of the way WordStar's menus work. In word processing, a **menu** is a list (not of dishes of food but) of commands available to you. WordStar has many separate menus. And, in addition to the menus, you can call up detailed **on-screen explanations** of almost every aspect of WordStar's operation.

You can set the level of help you get from menus. Levels of help range from the most basic—where the menus are rather complete and take up a relatively large part of the screen—to more advanced—where the menus are somewhat skimpier and leave more of the screen for your text—to the expert level—in which the menus virtually disappear (you can get them back if you need them). This is a feature that other programs may have copied by now, but in any case, WordStar introduced it.

In addition to the basic repertoire of word processing commands (move up, down, left, right; insert text here; delete letter, word, line; etc.), WordStar also lets you move blocks of text, insert text from a different file, return to a previously marked place, and find and replace a word or phrase.

You can find and/or replace a given piece of text just once, any specified number of times, or wherever it occurs in the file. You can have WordStar pause at each occurrence and ask you if you want to go ahead with the substitution. You can have the substitution done on whole words only. If you want, WordStar will ignore whether some or all of a word's letters are upper- or lowercase.

Formatting Features

You can have each line **justified** to both margins (so that the right—as well as the left—margin makes a straight vertical line). When this format is chosen, WordStar places the justifying spaces between letters as well as between words (if the printer can do that). Or you can use the more common "ragged right" format.

Page numbering (if desired) is automatic, and you can choose where to put the number on the page. The automatic printing of headers and footers on every page (if desired) is also possible. Lines can be centered automatically. All such commands can be inserted into the actual text, where they will be obeyed but not printed out.

WordStar can even hyphenate for you. It will find and mark good places to divide long words that fall at the ends of lines. Then it will query you in each instance, so you can decide whether to hyphenate or not, or to hyphenate at a different place in the word. If the text is changed or reformed so that those words no longer fall at the end of lines, WordStar will drop the hyphens. You can also put these **conditional hyphens** in yourself.

You can set tabs so that the decimal points of numbers in a column all line up directly below one another. And you can also set variable tabs—i.e., the distance between them can vary.

You can tell WordStar at any given point in a file to count the number of lines to the end of a page and, if there are less than a certain number (which you specify) to go on to the next page. This command is used to keep a table, chart, or group of lines on the same page, regardless of where it falls in the printout.

In addition to underlining, WordStar will produce **boldfacing, doublestriking,** superscripts ($E = MC^2$), subscripts (H_2O), and ~~strikeout~~ (useful for legal documents).

WordStar will print out on single sheets of paper (pausing after each one until you tell it to go on, so you can insert the next sheet) or on continuous-form paper. You can interrupt printout at any time, and you can also tell WordStar to print out just pages 18 to 25, for example.

Although WordStar can be extensively customized to your particular requirements, everything is initially preset at a convenient value (for example, single spacing, a top margin of 1/2 inch, a page length that fits 11-inch sheets of paper, etc.). These preset values are called **defaults.** Thanks to defaults, you can use WordStar without needing to learn how to set a value for every parameter.

With the more recent versions of WordStar (3.3 and later), you can even change many of the default settings, so that you don't have to change them each time you work. This lets you create one WordStar for writing letters, another for writing memos, and so on. (For a list of the defaults that can be changed, see the WordStar installation manual.)

On IBM PC or a PC compatible, versions from 3.3 on also let you reprogram the function keys to make them do different things. And if you have a PC or compatible with a color monitor, you can even choose what color you want the background and text to be. Since there are eight choices for each, you can create 56 different combinations (not counting green on green, white on white, and other pointless configurations).

MicroPro is a relatively responsive company and, unlike many others, is always improving its product and adapting it to the needs of its customers. This is an extremely important factor in choosing a word processing program.

3 A Taste of WordStar in One Hour

IF YOU WANT TO DIG into the nuts and bolts of WordStar immediately, just read the first five paragraphs of this chapter and then skip to Chapter 4. But if, like a lot of people, you enjoy trying things out and getting a feeling for them before you actually learn how they work, this chapter is for you. In it, you'll be walked through the writing of a business letter. I won't stop to explain why you're doing what you're doing—that's covered in the next chapter.

Installing WordStar

The first thing you should do when you get the WordStar **distribution disks** (the ones MicroPro sent you) is to make copies of them and put the originals away. Then you should run the WINSTALL program to customize WordStar to your terminal and printer.

WSU.COM is the name of the program MicroPro sent you. When WordStar is installed, another program called WS.COM is created. You need WS.COM on the disk to be able to run WordStar; WSU.COM (which stands for "WordStar Uninstalled") won't work.

The disk you actually use, with WS.COM on it, is called a **work disk.** (On some computers, WS.COM is "hidden" so that it doesn't show in the directory, even though it's on the disk.) You should also make a copy of this and put it in a safe place. Remember that the information on a disk is always worth more than the disk itself. So don't scrimp.

Opening Commands

Since computer systems are different, I leave it to you to get yours turned on with PC-DOS loaded into it. Once you see the A> at the left side of the screen, insert the WordStar disk. Then type **ws** (just those two letters) and press the ↵ key. Your disk drive will start making noise (by the way, never touch your drives when WordStar is working), and a menu will appear on your screen.

Type in the letter **D** (caps or lowercase, it makes no difference). The screen will change again. (There's a delay each time the screen changes. Sometimes WordStar will put the word WAIT on the screen.)

The cursor is now sitting at the end of a line that reads:

NAME OF FILE TO EDIT?

Type in:

formltr.doc

That's the name of the document, or file, that you'll be working on.

If you make a mistake typing, go back to correct it by using the key labeled **Del** (for "delete") in the lower right corner of the keyboard.

As you move backwards with Del, the letters you typed will disappear. Move back over the mistake and then type out the file name again. Once you have it right, hit ↵. The screen will change. When it settles down, the cursor will be under the left side of a new menu. Now you can begin writing.

Just type the letter that follows as if you were using a typewriter. One difference is that you don't have to use carriage returns at the end of each line. Don't try to match the line endings of the letter as it appears in this book with what you see on the screen. WordStar will automatically take any word that doesn't fit at the end of a line and start a new line with it. There are several places, though, where you should hit the ↵ key; I've marked them ↵.

If you make a mistake, go back to it with the 4 on the numeric keypad (which also has a ←). Then hit the 0 on the numeric keypad (which also says Ins). The words INSERT ON will disappear from the upper right corner of the screen, and you'll be able to type over the mistake. (There may be easier ways to do all these things, but this is just a *taste* of WordStar.)

The Spacebar and the tab key work just the way they do on a typewriter. The tab key is just to the left of the letter Q. It has two arrows, one pointing to the left, and one to the right. Don't be startled when the text begins to move up under the menu. Just keep on typing. And that's all you need to know for the moment.

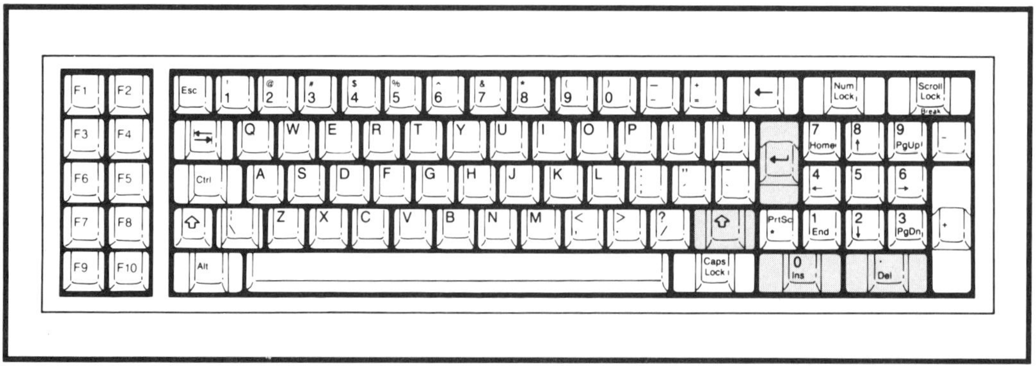

The Esc, Tab, Return, Shift, Ins, and Del keys

Here's what you should type:

.op↵

May 28, 1985↵

↵

↵

↵

Dear ______________,↵

↵

This form letter is in response to your form letter dated ______________. Your account number with me is ______________. Please refer to this number in all future correspondence.↵

↵

In recent months, unanticipated increases in my expenses have seriously clouded my cash flow picture. Unfortunately, I have no alternative but to ask you to share the burden of these higher costs with me. You'll be happy to know, however, that as one of my AAA creditors, you will continue to receive nominal payments, unlike many less highly rated accounts.↵

↵

NOTICE: Your creditor rating is up for review. Don't be alarmed. In most cases this is merely a formality.↵

↵

Thank you for your understanding in this matter.↵

↵

Yours truly,↵

↵

↵

↵

↵

↵

If you have already received payment, please disregard this notice.↵[1]

.pa↵

[1]Form letter © 1978 by Arthur Naiman.

Now type ^KD (that is, hold down the key marked Ctrl and press K and then D). If the screen changes, pay no attention to it, even if it happens between the ^K and the D. Just finish with the command.

As the screen says, WordStar is now saving the file named FORMLTR.DOC on disk, so you can call it up and work with it again at some time in the future. When the save is finished and the cursor is under the right side of the menu, hit P.

Now turn your printer on and make sure there's a sheet of paper in it. (If there's anything else you have to do to get your printer ready to print, now's the time to do it.) WordStar is asking you:

NAME OF FILE TO PRINT?

Type in:

formltr.doc

(Use the Del key to make corrections if you need to.) After the name is typed, hit the key marked Esc in the upper left corner of the keyboard. WordStar will print the letter out.

So—you've opened a WordStar file, edited it, saved it, and printed it out, and I'll bet it didn't even take you an hour.

4 Getting Started Editing with WordStar

NOW THAT YOU'VE HAD A TASTE of what WordStar is like to work with, it's time to create some text of your own. If you didn't work your way through Chapter 3, go back and read the first five paragraphs. You may also want to refer to the keyboard diagram in Chapter 3.

The first thing you see when you type **ws** ↵ to enter WordStar is a screen that gives you information about your copy of WordStar. It shows you the version number and the serial number, along with some copyright and installation (i.e., customization) information. This display lasts for a few seconds, and then the **opening menu** appears. (If you're using WordStar Version 3.2, this menu is titled **no-file menu.**)

```
not editing
            <<<    O P E N I N G   M E N U    >>>
- - -Preliminary Commands- - -    | - -File Commands- - | -System Commands-
L  Change logged disk drive       |                     |  R  Run a program
F  File directory off (ON)        | P  Print a file     |  X  EXIT to system
H  Set help level                 |                     |
 - - -Commands to Open a file- - -| E  RENAME a file    | -WordStar Options-
     D  Open a document file      | O  COPY a file      |  M  Run MailMerge
     N  Open a non-document file  | Y  DELETE a file    |  S  Run SpellStar
DIRECTORY of disk A:
 PRINT.TST        WS.COM     WSMSGS.OVR     WSOVLY1.OVR
```

The Opening Menu

As I mentioned in Chapter 2, this is called a *menu* because you can choose from the commands listed the way you choose from the dishes on a restaurant's menu. (In earlier versions, WordStar called this the "no-file" menu because you haven't yet picked a file to work on.)

If you've been working directly through from Chapter 3, you'll have noticed that ^KD also puts you here on the opening menu.

At the very bottom of the screen you'll see a row of numbers 1 through 10 with labels like "Help" and "Indent". The numbers refer to the ten function keys at the left side of the keyboard, and the labels remind you what each key does. For now you can just ignore this information. (If you're using wordStar Version 3.2, this line doesn't appear on the screen.)

Creating a New File

Since you now want to "open a document file" (we'll ignore for the moment what a "non-document file" is), press the **D** key on your keyboard (capital D or lowercase d—it doesn't make any difference). Another display, the **D command display,** appears on the screen. (It's not a menu because it doesn't give you a choice of commands.)

```
D      not editing

   Use this command to create a new document file,
   or to initiate alteration of an existing document file.

      A file name is 1–8 letters/digits, a period,
      and an optional 0–3 character type.
      File name may be preceded by a disk drive letter A–D
      and colon, otherwise current logged disk is used.

^S=delete character    ^Y=delete entry    ^F=File directory
^D=restore character   ^R=Restore entry   ^U=cancel command

   NAME OF FILE TO EDIT? ▲

partial DIRECTORY of disk A:      ^Z=scroll up
   PRINT.TST           WS.COM     WSMSGS.OVR     WSOVLY1.OVR
```

The D Command Display

The D command display is all pretty understandable (although I might be tempted to substitute "re-edit" for "initiate alteration of," myself). Still, a little clarification can't hurt.

The words "not editing" at the top simply mean: "so far you're not editing any file." The D display asks you for the name of a file to edit.

Entering the File Name

There's no distinction between caps and lowercase letters in a **file name.** If you type in lowercase letters, WordStar will interpret them as caps. As the menu tells you, a file name can be from one to eight characters (letters or numbers) long; depending on your version of WordStar, some punctuation marks and symbols can't be used. If you type in a file name that includes an illegal character, the screen will say INVALID FILE NAME, and you'll get a chance to type in a new one.

File names have two parts: the name itself and a three-character code called the **extension, extent,** or **type** (because it's used to indicate what type of file it is). Some examples of types are DOC (for "DOCument"), BAK (for "BAcKup"), TXT (for "TeXT"), LET (for "LETter"), and LST (for "LiST"). You can make up any type you want to distinguish categories of files (but WordStar won't edit a file with the type BAK—you have to change the type first). You can also leave the type off. Types are separated from the main file name by a period.

On the IBM PC there are six file names you must avoid because they have special meaning for PC-DOS. They are:

CON
AUX
COM1
LPT1
PRN
NUL

Here are some examples of valid file names:

CHAP1.DOC
CHAP1.BAK
CHAP2
3
LAUNDRY.LST
DEARJOHN.LET
JBOND.007
DOOBEDOO.ZXZ

If you want, you can also put a single letter followed by a colon (**A:**, **B:**, etc.) in front of the file name. This specifies which drive the disk with the file is on. If you don't have such a letter in front of the file name, WordStar will look for the file on (and put the file back onto) the logged drive—which is A unless you've changed it.

Halfway down the D display are two lines of commands. They're there to help you if you make a mistake entering the file name. In this context, ^S lets you erase characters going backwards (towards the left), one at a time. (One character means one space, regardless of what's on it—a letter, a number, a symbol, a carriage return, or just a blank space.) The Del key has the same effect as ^S and is probably easier to use. You can take your pick. ^Y kills the whole entry and puts you back on the first space. Those are the commands you're most likely to need.

At the bottom of the screen is the **directory**—the list of files on the logged disk. There may not be room to list all of them, but if you want to see more, use ^Z to bring the rest of them into view.

OK—now type in your file name. You can use any name you want, but I'm going to be calling the file we create PRACTICE.DOC, so you probably should too. Why make trouble for yourself? When you've finished typing PRACTICE.DOC, hit ↵.

If a file named PRACTICE.DOC doesn't exist on your disk, WordStar puts the words:

NEW FILE

on the screen for a few seconds. If you meant to edit an already existing file (FORMLTR.DOC, for example), this would tell you that you typed the name in wrong. In this case, of course, we are intentionally beginning work on a new file.

After the words NEW FILE disappear, a new menu appears on the screen. It's called the **main menu**.

It might be more accurate to call the opening menu (the first one shown in this chapter) the "main" menu, since all the other menus and command displays flow from it, and to call this the "main editing menu." But, in another sense, this really *is* the main menu, since you spend the most of your time working under it. It's the main menu in terms of use.

```
     A:PRACTICE.DOC    PAGE 1   LINE 1   COL 01              INSERT ON

                  < < <         M A I N   M E N U          > > >

   - -Cursor Movement- -        |  -Delete-  |    -Miscellaneous-      |    -Other  Menus-
^S char left    ^D char right   | ^G  char   | ^I  Tab      ^B Reform  |    (from Main only)
^A word left    ^F word right   | DEL chr lf | ^V  INSERT ON/OFF       | ^J Help      ^K Block
^E line up      ^X line down    | ^T  word rt| ^L  Find/Replce again   | ^Q Quick     ^P Print
          - -Scrolling- -       | ^Y  line   | RETURN End paragraph    | ^O Onscreen
^Z line up      ^W line down    |            | ^N  Insert a RETURN     |
^C screen up    ^R screen down  |            | ^U  Stop a command      |

L    !    !    !    !    !    !    !    !    !----!--------R
▲
```

The Main Menu

The Status Line

The very top line is called the **status line.** On the left is the name of the file you're editing, which in this case is A:PRACTICE.DOC ("A:" because you're logged onto drive A). Your cursor is on page 1, line 1, in the first space (or column) of the line. Type in any one letter. Now COL indicates 02. Type in more text until COL indicates 10.

Now hit ^S. Here, under the main menu, ^S moves the cursor left but does *not* delete text. You can also move left by hitting the 4 on the numeric keypad (also labeled with a left arrow). Notice how the number after COL changes each time you move the cursor left.

^D (or alternatively, 6 on the numeric keypad) moves the cursor one character (one space) to the right. As you try that, you will see the column number increase. But it won't go higher than 10, because there is no text beyond that.

The IBM PC keyboard has an **auto-repeat** feature. If you hold a key (or combination of keys) down, the character or command will repeat until you release it. Try holding down ^D. You'll see the cursor move steadily to the right.

On the right side of the status line are the words INSERT ON. I'll explain what that means in a couple of pages, but for now all you need to know is that WordStar can work in two modes—insertion and write-over. The 0 on the numeric keypad (also labeled **Ins**) switches you back and forth between them. Try hitting Ins. The words INSERT ON have disappeared. Now hit it again. You're back in insertion mode, as indicated by the words INSERT ON on the status line. **^V** has the same effect as Ins.

Moving the Cursor

The first column of the main menu begins with the commands for moving the cursor. You've already experimented with ^S (back one character) and ^D (forward one character). Now type a few words separated by spaces. **^A** moves the cursor back one *word* (that is, to the beginning of the first word to the left, or to the beginning of the word the cursor is in the middle of). Play with ^A (you should experiment with each new command).

^F moves the cursor forward one word, that is, to the first letter of the next word to the right. These four commands (^S, ^D, ^A, and ^F) will get you anywhere you want to go on a line very quickly.

Now you can see why you might want to use the control character commands, ^S and ^D, even though the forward and backward arrows on the numeric keypad are easier to remember and require only a single keystroke. With your hand positioned over S and D, you can easily reach A and F as well. This lets you move flexibly across a line of text by letters and words.

But what if you want to move the cursor to another line? One way to do that is with the key labeled ↵. This "forces a **line feed**"—that is, it moves the cursor to the start of the next line regardless of whether there's any text on it. If there isn't, you'll get a blank line at this point. If there is, the line you were on will be broken, as at the end of a paragraph, right where you hit ↵.

Hit ↵. Notice that the cursor is now on the second line, and LINE at the top of the screen now reads 02. But usually you want to move down without inserting blank lines into your text. And, of course, if you just use ↵, you'll keep moving down the screen, adding blank lines, and never actually get to the next line of text. So there are commands that move you up and down over existing text without changing it.

But before you can learn to use them, you'll need more than one line of text to work with. Actually, about 24 lines will be ideal. To generate them, you can do one of the following:

1. Type in gibberish. If your keyboard has auto-repeat, all you have to do is hold down any key or keys, inserting spaces every now and then.
2. If you went through the last chapter and typed in the letter, hit ^KQ, then Y, then D when the opening menu comes up on the screen, and enter FORMLTR.DOC as the file name on the D command display.
3. Type in something of your own, either serious or not.
4. Type in the pocm below. Be sure to hit ⟵┘ at the end of each line, so WordStar won't run the lines together. To get a blank line between stanzas, hit ⟵┘ twice in a row. To center the title, space over from the left margin (there's another way to do this, but we're not ready for it yet).

For Anne Gregory

"Never shall a young man,
Thrown into despair,
By those great honey-colored
Ramparts at your ear,
Love you for yourself alone
And not your yellow hair."

"But I can get a hair-dye
And set such color there,
Brown, or black, or carrot,
That young men in despair
May love me for myself alone
And not my yellow hair."

"I heard an old religious man
But yesternight declare
That he had found a text to prove
That only God, my dear,
Could love you for yourself alone
And not your yellow hair."

—William Butler Yeats

At some point while you were typing, the text began to move up the screen, and eventually began disappearing under the menu. WordStar automatically does this to make room for you. Now let's look at the ways you can move through the text yourself.

^**E** will move the cursor up a line. Use it to get back to the title. ^**X** will move you down a line. Use it to get back to the line with Yeats' name on it. You can also move up or down a line with the 8 and 2 on the numeric keypad.

^E, ^X, ^S, ^D, ^A, and ^F were not chosen arbitrarily. If you look at the first four of these keys on your keyboard, you'll see that they form a diamond, with each letter pointing in the direction it moves the cursor.

Furthermore, ^A is to the left of ^S, since it moves the cursor even further to the left than ^S does (a word rather than a character). And ^F is to the right of ^D, since it moves the cursor further to the right. (Learning the commands ^D and ^S makes it easier to learn and remember the other WordStar commands that are logically related to them.)

There are two additional cursor-movement keys on the numeric keypad that may come in handy. **Home**—as in "home base"—moves the cursor to the upper left corner of the screen. **End** puts the cursor at the bottom of the screen, directly below its original position. The corresponding control-key commands are quite complicated.

Scrolling

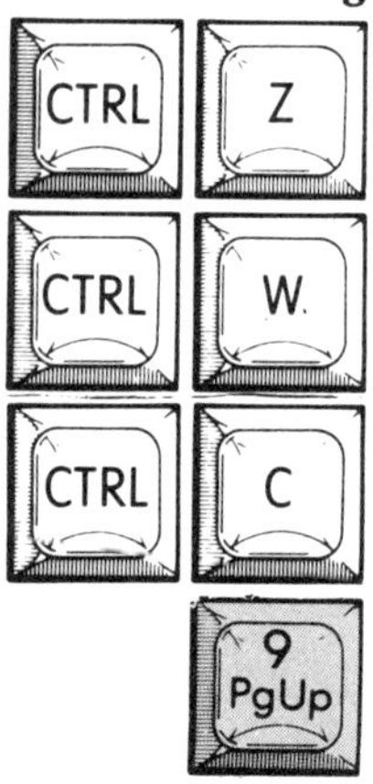

On the left side of ^E and ^X on your keyboard are ^W and ^Z. On the right side are ^R and ^C. These two pairs of commands are used to move the text, rather than the cursor, up and down. This is called **scrolling.** (Scrolling is what WordStar did when it ran out of room for the poem and started tucking it under the menu.)

^**Z** scrolls text up a line and ^**W** scrolls text down a line. There's a potential confusion here, because moving the *text* up is like moving the *cursor* down, and vice versa. You should experiment with ^E, ^X, ^Z, and ^W until you have a feel for what each of them does.

It's also possible to move text up and down a screenful (rather than just a line) at a time. ^**C** moves text up a screenful, and ^**R**

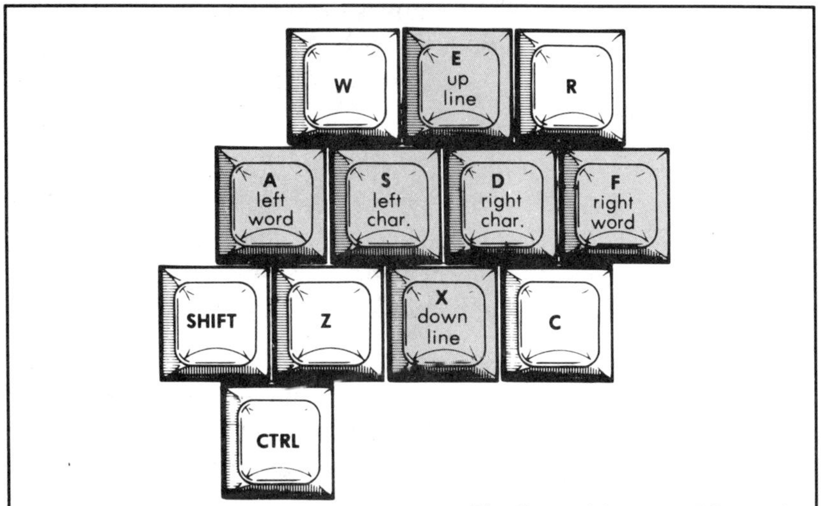

The Cursor-Movement Diamond

down a screenful (actually, 3/4 of a screenful, so you have some overlap from one screenful to the next). On the numeric keypad the keys labeled **PgDn** (9) ad **PgUp** (3) duplicate ^C and ^R. Again, their advantage is that they require only one keystroke.

With ^Z and ^W, the cursor moves with the text until it hits the top or bottom of the screen. It then remains on the top or bottom line. With ^C and ^R, the cursor does not move with the text. It remains where it was before you began scrolling.

Deleting Text

That covers the basic commands for moving the cursor and moving the text. The second column of the main menu covers deletion. There are two ways to delete a single character. The **Del** key removes the character directly to the left of the cursor. **^G** erases the character directly above the cursor.

If you find this confusing, just use one or the other. But, as you become accustomed to having both commands at your disposal, you'll see that two commands are more convenient than one.

If you use ^G on the last space of a line, it will delete the carriage return at the end of the line and join it with the line below.

^T will kill a whole word if the cursor is on the first letter, or whatever remains of a word if the cursor is farther in. Basically, ^T erases everything up to the start of the next word, including the punctuation and/or the space immediately following the word.

^Y removes the whole line that the cursor is on. The line below it (if any) moves up to fill the gap.

Miscellaneous Commands

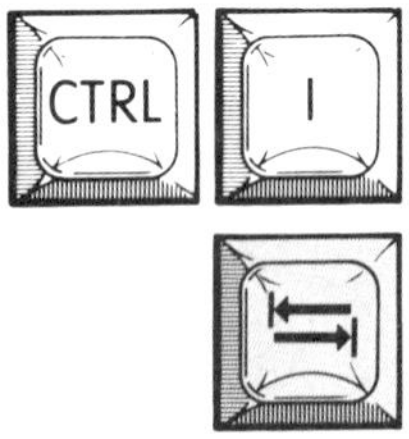

The third column in the main menu covers miscellaneous commands that are frequently used to edit a file. **^I** is the equivalent of the TAB key on a typewriter, only more flexible. The PC has a special tab key (just to the left of the letter Q) marked with right and left arrows. Despite the left arrow, this key won't tab to the left because WordStar has no command for a backward tab.

The line at the bottom of the menu, which looks sort of like a ruler, shows you where the tab stops are currently set. Each one is marked by a !. What the tab key does depends on whether you're in insertion mode or write-over mode.

In insert mode, the tab key inserts as many spaces as it takes to get the cursor to the next tab stop, and pushes all the text beyond the cursor forward that many spaces. In write-over mode, the tab key moves the cursor over existing text to the next tab stop without inserting any spaces.

If there are no more tab stops on a line, the tab key will move the cursor to the first tab stop on the next line. (How to change tab stops is covered in Chapter 9.)

When you make insertions and deletions, the text on your screen can begin to look pretty messy. **^B** will reform a paragraph from the cursor on so that it looks the way it would if you had just typed it in directly, with each line filled and with the text that doesn't fit on a line automatically moved down to the next line. ^B can also be used to see how a text will look with different margins, different line spacing, etc. You have to use ^B for each paragraph you want to reform, unless you use **^QQ ^B** (see page 41). If ^B stops, it may be because of hyphen help (see pages 80–81 for more details).

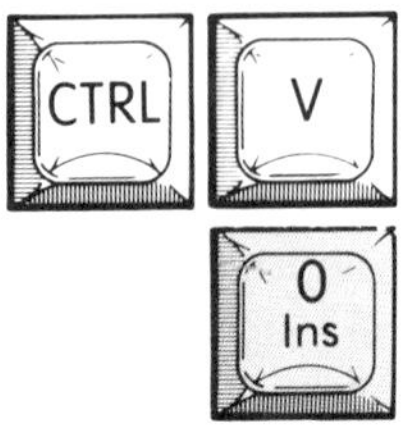

I talked a little about **^V** above. The zero key on the numeric keypad (also labeled **Ins**) has the same effect as ^V and is easier to remember and use. This command switches you back and forth between insert mode and write-over mode. **Insert mode** is the default; that is, if you never hit Ins or ^V, you'll always be in insert mode, and the words INSERT ON will appear on the right side of the status line.

Put your cursor between two words in the middle of any line. Now start typing. What you type is inserted between those two words, and everything after it on the line is pushed right.

Now, without moving the cursor, hit Ins. The words INSERT ON disappear, indicating that you are now in **write-over** mode. Start typing. Instead of the text being inserted, it's written over (and replaces) what was previously there.

Ins acts as a **toggle,** which means if insertion mode was on, Ins turns it off. If it was off, Ins turns it on. Normally you'll be working in insertion mode, but sometimes it's more convenient to hit Ins and just write over a chunk of text, rather than to delete it and then insert the new text in its place.

^L is used to repeat the last find or replace command used. (These commands are the subject of Chapter 7.)

The ↵ key inserts a **hard carriage return** into the text. That is, no matter what place on the line that hard return occurs, WordStar will start a new line. A **soft carriage return** is what WordStar puts into the text when it reaches the end of a line. If you delete a word from that line and then reform it with ^B, the soft carriage return will shift to the new end of the line. However, if you put a hard carriage return at any place in a file, it stays there until you delete it.

Normally, you use ↵ to indicate the end of a paragraph (not a line), to insert a blank line, or to keep lines of text from running together (as for titles, or lines you want centered).

There is also another way to insert a hard carriage return— **^N**. The difference is that with ^N the cursor stays in front of the carriage return, instead of moving down to the start of the next line. Another difference is that if your text is being printed out double spaced, ↵ will give you two carriage returns. ^N, however, always gives you only one carriage return, no matter what line spacing you're using.

When a line on the screen ends in a soft carriage return (so that the line break can move to a different place if you reformat the text), a blank space appears in the last column on the right. If a line ends with a hard carriage return, inserted by ↵ or ^N (so that there will be a line break there no matter how the text is changed), the < symbol appears in the last space.

There are several other symbols that appear in the last column. They're called **flag characters,** and +, P, ?, and – are the most common. + indicates that the line it's at the end of continues onto the next line—that is, that line and the next are really all one line, but because of the limited width of the screen, they are displayed as two. P is described in Chapter 9 and ? and – in Chapter 10. An on-screen explanation of all flag characters is accessed with the ^JF command, which is described in Chapter 5.

The last command in the third column of the main menu is **^U**. If you ask WordStar to do something and then change your mind, ^U will stop the command (or commands) being executed.

*** INTERRUPTED *** Press ESCAPE Key

will appear on the screen and you'll have to hit the **Esc** key to continue working.

The last column of the main menu tells you how to get to other menus, and how to adjust the amount of help you get from the menus to match your level of competence with WordStar. (You learn about all that in the next chapter.)

At the bottom of the main menu is the **ruler line** (the letters L and R with the dashes and exclamation marks in between). **L** and **R** stand for left and right margins. Chapter 9 tells you how to change them from their default values (1 and 60 on a screen that's 64 characters wide; 1 and 65 on a screen that's 80 characters wide).

Below the ruler line is the area where the text you create appears. Before going on to the next chapter, it would be a good idea for you to practice the commands presented in this chapter until you feel fairly comfortable with them.

This will also give you a chance to see whether you prefer moving the cursor with the control key commands or with the numeric keypad. The chart in Appendix D shows the keys on the numeric keypad and thc commands they execute.

Saving a File

If you want to stop for a while, and continue learning about WordStar later, you should save the file you now have in the workspace—even if only to save yourself retyping some text to work with later. (However, the trustees of the Yeats estate asked me to remind you that making a copy of it for any purpose other than your own personal use is illegal.)

Remember that when you load a file to edit it, WordStar doesn't move the file from the disk into memory; it makes a copy of the disk file and puts the copy in memory. The original file on the disk remains unchanged—until you save the version that's in memory. Unless you do that, there's no permanent record of the changes you've made. They all disappear when you turn off the computer.

There are three WordStar commands that save files:

- ^KD (for "Done")
- ^KX (for "eXit")
- ^KS (for "reSume")

^KD (you hold down the control key and type k immediately followed by d) saves the file you're working on and returns you to the opening menu (the first one shown in this chapter).

If you pause more than half a second between the ^K and the D (it doesn't have to be a ^D, by the way; a regular d is OK too), the screen will change and a new menu will come up. As I mentioned when we used this command at the end of Chapter 3, hitting D will still execute the command. In fact, you'll see the ^KD command listed on this new menu.

^KX saves the file and takes you out of WordStar into the operating system. If you're going to stop using WordStar completely, it's the command to use.

You can also save a file and continue editing it by hitting **^KS.** This saves the file and returns you to it, with the cursor at the beginning. If you want the cursor back where it was before you saved the file, hit ^QP as your first command upon returning.

It's a good idea to use ^KS frequently when working on real files (not practice ones like these). Then if something happens—like a power failure or computer crash—you'll only lose the work you did since the last time you used ^KS to save. It's also essential to keep multiple backup files on separate disks. You have to exit from WordStar to do that.

Another way you can lose work is by not keeping track of how full your disk is. You should check it regularly (by hitting R under the opening menu and then running the CHKDSK program). If CHKSDK doesn't work, it may be becase the CHKDSK program hasn't been copied from the PC-DOS disk onto your work disk. You may want to stop and do this.

You should keep at least twice as much empty space on a disk as your largest file; otherwise, under certain circumstances, it may be impossible to save the file you've been working on. (A discussion of the dangers and benefits of large files, including other ways to check how large a file is and how full the disk is, is found in Chapter 8.)

You can also leave WordStar without saving the file you've been working on. A common use is when you were just looking at a file and didn't make any changes in it. Another use is when you've hopelessly messed up the version you're working on and just want to dump it. The command for this is **^KQ.** As a safety precaution, if changes have been made in the file, WordStar asks:

ABANDON EDITED VERSION OF FILE B:FILENAME ? (Y/N):

You must type Y (for "yes") in order for the command to be executed. ^KQ puts you back at the opening menu.

Remember to remove your disk *before* turning off the computer but *after* WordStar has finished saving the last file. In fact, for safety's sake, make sure you're out of WordStar before you remove the disk by using either ^KX or ^KD, followed by X, to get back to the operating system.

5 The Control-Character Menus

IN CHAPTERS 3 AND 4, I've pretty much restricted myself to WordStar's basic menu. As a result, almost all the commands I discussed there were one letter long. But if you look at your WordStar reference card, you'll see that most of the commands on it are two letters long. These two-letter commands are accessed through five different submenus of the main menu. Because the main menu is concerned with editing, I call these other menus **editing menus.** And because you hit a control character to get to each of these editing menus, I also call them **control-character menus.** There are five control-character menus: ^Q, ^K, ^O, ^P, and ^J.

The ^Q Menu

If you are re-entering WordStar, type ws, then d, and then a file name to get to the main menu. (The file name may be either old or new; you can "open" an existing file as well as a new one.) Now type ^Q. This causes a new menu, the **^Q menu,** to appear on the screen. (Q stands for "quick," by the way, because the ^Q menu offers you more powerful commands than the main menu in the areas of cursor movement, deletion, and global substitution. These commands help you do things more quickly.)

Now hit the key marked **Esc.** This takes you back to the main menu. Esc returns you to the main menu from any of the control-character menus. (From the command displays, Esc returns you to the opening menu. More on this in Chapter 8.)

Actually, not only Esc but any key that's not a command listed on a given menu will terminate that menu on the screen and return you to the main menu. You can use, for example, a letter, a number, or, as is indicated at the bottom of each control-character menu, the Spacebar.

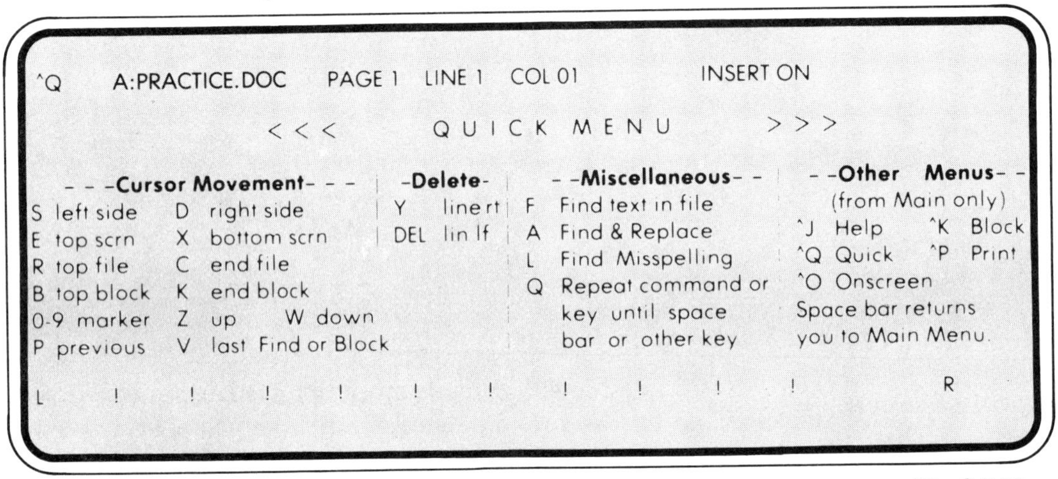

The ^Q Menu

To get back to the ^Q menu, hit ^Q again. Like the main menu, the ^Q menu has a status line at its top that tells you what file you're working on, where you are in it, and whether you're in insertion mode. Unlike the main menu, it also has the notation ^Q at the beginning of the status line.

All the commands listed on this menu can be ordered from the main menu by preceding them with ^Q. So, for example, ^QS with the main menu at the top of the screen has exactly the same effect as S does with the ^Q menu at the top of the screen. In either case, the same sequence of characters is required.

To avoid confusion, I'll put the ^Q (and other **prefixes**) in front of each command whenever I discuss it; remember that you don't need to type in the prefix when it's already at the top of the screen. If you do, WordStar will execute ^QQ (in this case), a command which means "repeat the next command," which is probably not what you want to do.

Also, you don't need to hold down the control key for the second letter of the command, because anything you type under the ^Q menu, including regular characters, is interpreted as a command (just as if it were the second letter of a two-letter command).

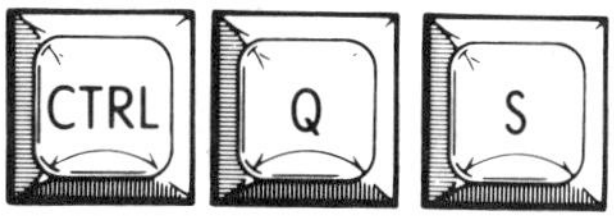

^**QS** moves the cursor all the way to the left end of the line it's on. ^**QD** moves it all the way to the right. If you're working with lines wider than 80 characters and you use ^QD to move the cursor off the right edge of the screen, the line the cursor is on will shift over about 60 characters (that is, you'll see the next 60 characters of text on the right as the first 60 characters on the line disappear off the left edge of the screen).

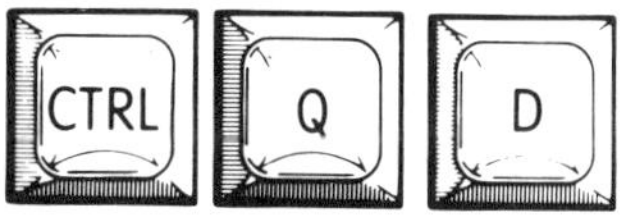

About one second later, the rest of the lines will follow suit. Hit ^QD again, and you'll get another 60 characters, and so on to the maximum line length of 240 characters (or, with word wrap off, about 32,000 characters). ^QS will return the cursor to column 1, and the first 80 characters of the line will immediately appear on the screen.

^**QE** moves the cursor to the top line of the screen, keeping it as close as possible to the same place on the line. ^**QX** moves it to the same place on the last line on the screen. (The **End** key, number 1 in the numeric keypad, has the same effect as ^QX.)

These four commands weren't chosen arbitrarily. Look back at the cursor-movement diamond in Chapter 4 and you'll see that just as ^S moves the cursor one space to the left, ^QS moves it all the way to the left; just as ^X moves the cursor down one line, ^QX moves it all the way down; etc. Many ^Q commands are basically exaggerations of simpler commands.

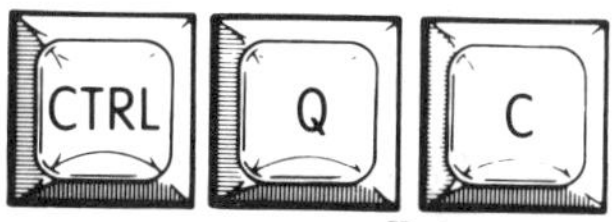

For example, ^C moves the text up a screenful; ^**QC** moves the text all the way up and puts the cursor at the end of the file. ^R moves the text down a screenful; ^**QR** moves the text all the way down, putting the cursor at the beginning of the file. But if the cursor is near the end of a long file, saving the file with ^KS may be a faster way to get the cursor to the beginning. In earlier versions of WordStar, ^KS was also better because it created less of a risk of running out of disk space than ^QR. (This is discussed fully in Appendix A.) Both ^QR and ^QC can be given with a single keystroke (rather than three) by using the function keys at the left side of the keyboard. Key F10 duplicates ^QC and moves the cursor to the end of the file. Key F9 has the same effect as ^QR.

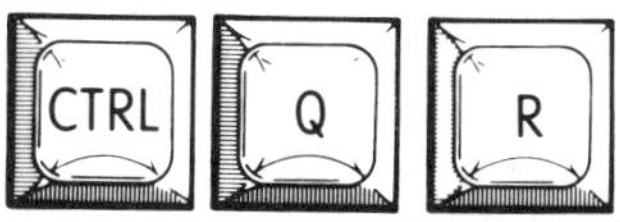

^Z scrolls the text up one line each time you hit it; ^**QZ** scrolls the text up *continuously,* until you order it to stop. ^**QW** scrolls the text down continuously. You can control the speed at which it scrolls by hitting **any number** from 1 (the fastest) to 9 (the slowest). You hit the number while the scrolling is going on, and you can change the speed as often as you want. The beginning speed is 3—that is, relatively fast. To stop the scrolling, hit any other key (for example, the Spacebar).

^QB and ^QK have to do with blocks of text that are marked off, moved, deleted, etc. This subject is covered in the next chapter. ^QV is discussed both in the next chapter and the one following.

WordStar gives you an opportunity to mark up to ten different places in a file, and then return the cursor to them whenever you want. You mark a place by typing **^K followed by a number** (0 to 9). The marker shows up in the text as <**n**> (where "n" stands for the number of the marker). The place marker will not print out, and the cursor skips over it. (It's also possible to "hide" it, so it won't show up even on the screen. There's a safety reason for doing this, which is discussed under ^KY in the next chapter.)

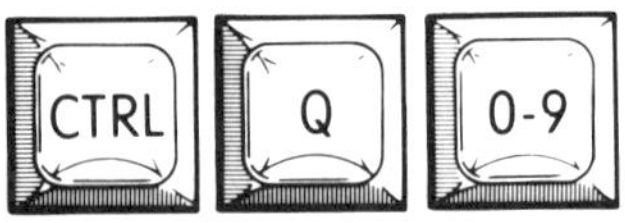

To move the cursor to a marked place, hit **^Q followed by the number of the marker** you want to move to (or, if you are already under the ^Q menu, just type the number).

^QP is a very useful command; it moves the cursor to where it was *before* the last command. This is obviously most helpful after commands that move the cursor some distance, for example, after saving a file with ^KS and reforming long paragraphs with ^B.

Under the **^Q** menu, **Y** deletes all of the line to the right of (i.e., after) the cursor. You can also hit ^Q followed by Y while under the main menu, of course, and get the same effect. The menu indicates that ^Q followed by Del will delete all of the line to the left of (i.e., before) the cursor. On the IBM PC, you'll have to substitute the backspace key for the Del key. (The backspace key—labeled with a left arrow—is just above the ↵ key.)

^QF and ^QA are covered in Chapter 7. ^QL is a SpellStar command and is covered in Chapter 13.

As I mentioned above, **^QQ** orders WordStar to repeat the *next* command entered. As with ^QW and ^QZ, you can control the rate at which the command is repeated by typing in any number from

1 (fastest) to 9 (slowest) while the command is being repeated. (Starting speed is 3.) To stop the command from repeating, just hit any character other than a number. ^QQ is particularly useful with ^B. **^QQ ^B** will reform every paragraph from the cursor to the end of the document without requiring you to keep repeating the ^B command (unless hyphen-help is on). After ^QQ ^B has finished, hit Esc to continue editing.

At the bottom of the ^Q menu is the ruler line, showing the location of the left and right margins and the tabs.

The ^K Menu

Like the ^Q menu, the **^K menu** offers enhancements of the main menu, but it specializes in the areas of file handling, and moving, copying, and deleting blocks of text (K stands for "blocK").

To get from any control-letter menu to any other, you have to go through the main menu. So to get from the ^Q menu to the ^K menu, hit Esc and then ^K (you have to wait for WordStar to finish writing the main menu before the ^K menu will appear). The screen will now look like this:

```
^K  A:PRACTICE.DOC  PAGE 1  LINE 1  COL 01          INSERT ON

              < < <      B L O C K   M E N U      > > >

-Saving Files-    -Block Operations-    -File Operations-         -Other Menus-
S Save & resume | B Begin  K End      R  Read    P  Print       (from Main only)
D Save done     | H Hide / Display    O  Copy    E  Rename   ^J Help     ^K Block
X Save & exit   | C Copy   Y Delete   J  Delete              ^Q Quick    ^P Print
Q Abandon file  | V Move   W Write  | -Disk Operations-      | ^O Onscreen
-Place Markers- | N Column on (OFF) | L Change logged disk   | Space bar returns
0 9 set/hide 0 9|                   | F Directory on (OFF)   | you to Main Menu.

L    !    !    !    !    !    !----!----!----!----!----------R
```

The ^K Menu

You know this is the ^K menu because it says so at the start of the status line. The first column lists the four commands that save or abandon files and were discussed at the end of the last chapter. At the bottom are the ten optional place markers I dealt with a few pages ago while covering the ^Q commands that move the cursor to them.

The second column (and ^**KR** in the third column) deal with moving and deleting blocks of text, which is sometimes called **electronic cut and paste.** This is the subject of the next chapter.

The other commands in the third column have to do with file handling and related disk operations, and are covered in Chapter 8—except for ^KP, which has to do with printing out and is covered in Chapter 11.

The ^O Menu
The ^P Menu

The ^O menu has to do with on-screen formatting and will be discussed in Chapter 9, which is devoted to that subject. The ^P menu has to do with inserting print-control commands into the text and will be covered in Chapter 10.

The ^J Menu

The **^J menu** offers a series of fairly comprehensive on-screen explanations of various areas, and also lets you control how much information you want displayed in the menus. The less there is, the more text you can have displayed on the screen at any one time, and the faster WordStar will run.

Esc to the main menu and then hit ^J; your screen will now look like this:

```
^J  A:PRACTICE.DOC  PAGE 1   LINE 1   COL 01           INSERT ON

                <<<        H E L P   M E N U        >>>

                                        |                       |  - -Other Menus- -
H  Display & set the help level         |  S  Status line       |   (from Main only)
B  Paragraph reform (CONTROL-B)         |  R  Ruler line        |  ^J  Help      ^K Block
F  Flags in right-most column           |  M  Margins & Tabs    |  ^Q  Quick     ^P Print
D  Dot commands, print controls         |  P  Place markers     |  ^O  Onscreen
                                        |  V  Moving text       |  Space bar returns
                                                                |  you to Main Menu.
L- - - -!- - - -!- - - -!- - - -!- - - -!- - - -!- - - -!- - - -!- - - -!- - - -!- - - - - - R
```

The ^J Menu

First let's cover the commands that generate on-screen explanations. These include all the commands on the ^J menu except ^JH. Some of these explanations are quite extensive, showing as many as six consecutive screenfuls of information. Let's look at them in order:

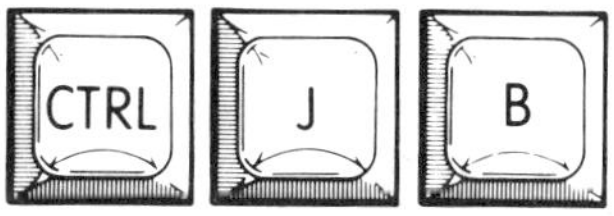

^JB gives you three screenfuls on paragraph reforming and on how to deal with the automatic hyphenation feature when you reform text. Once you've started this sequence (and most others), all you have to do to call up the next screenful of information is to hit any key. You can interrupt the sequence and return to the main editor by hitting ^U followed by Esc.

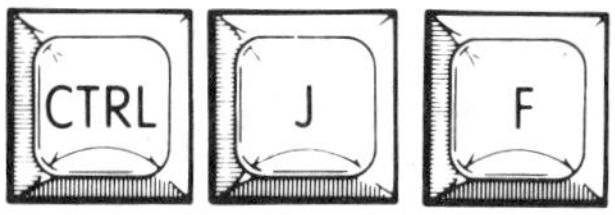

^JF explains the meaning of flags—the markers that appear in the last column on the right side of your screen (the most common ones are < and +). Since ^JF only takes one screenful to do this, when you press the Spacebar (or any key at all), you'll be returned to the main menu.

(By the way, it's impossible to get from a ^J on-screen explanation directly back to the ^J menu. If you want to go from one set of explanations to another, you have to return to the main menu, hit ^J again, and then the letter that will give you the explanation you want.)

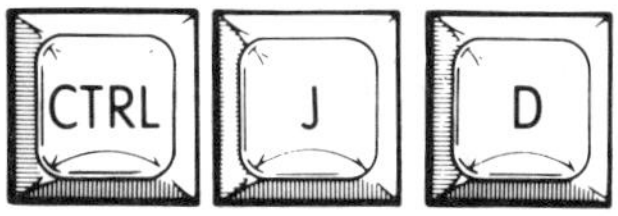

^JD provides six screenfuls of information on print features and dot commands, including a three-screenful list of dot commands, a list of special characters that can be used in headers and footers, and a list of dot commands used with the optional MailMerge program. Because there are so many screenfuls, WordStar lets you abort the ^JD series at various points (which are indicated on the screen) with a ^U command.

^JS gives you two screenfuls that explain the various notations that occur on the status line (the line that's always at the top of the screen). **^JR** gives you one screenful on what the markings on the ruler line mean, and how to change the values they stand for.

^JM offers a screenful on margins, followed by one on line-spacing and justification, another on tab stops, a fourth on the best way to set up a table with columns of data, and a final screenful on the easiest way to enter text in outline form.

^JP provides two screenfuls about marking blocks. **^JV** tells you how to move a block of text. **^JI** gives you a two-screenful summary of some common editing commands. (WordStar version 3.2 doesn't list ^JI on the menu.)

Now—WordStar lets you change the amount of information that's displayed on the menus. The function key **F1** gets you to the menu that does that. (The note "1 HELP" at the bottom of the screen is a reminder of that.) You can use ^JH to get to the same menu, but that requires three keystrokes rather than one. As the ^JH menu tells you, your present help level is 3, which means you are getting all the information available.

Level 2 kills all of the main menu except for the status line and the ruler line, giving you more room for your text. Level 1 does the same for the ^Q, ^K, ^O, ^P, and ^J menus (although all the sub-^J menus—the screenfuls of information and the ^JH menu for changing help levels—remain).

Remember that you can also suppress the control-character menus, without changing the help level, by simply typing the second letter of the command within two seconds of the first. Then the command will execute immediately and return you to the main menu without ever displaying the control-character menu.

Level 0 suppresses the explanations on the ^JH menu and on the opening command displays. You should change the help level and move around from one menu to another to see how each level affects the menus and on-screen explanations. Don't be afraid of getting lost for lack of information you still need; you can always get back to level 3 by getting to the main menu (no control character in the upper left corner), then hitting F1 (or ^JH), and then 3 (no ↵ is necessary). Even at level 0, the ^JH menu looks like this:

```
^JH    A:PRACTICE.DOC    PAGE 1   LINE 1   COL 01          INSERT ON

CURRENT HELP LEVEL IS 0

ENTER Space OR NEW HELP LEVEL (0, 1, 2, or 3): ▲
```

The ^JH Menu at Level 0

6 Moving and Deleting Blocks of Text

MANY EXPERIENCED WRITERS work by:

- typing up a draft of whatever they're working on;
- cutting it up; and
- pasting (or, more usually, taping) the pieces together in a new order.

Word processors let you do this sort of **electronic cut and paste** much more quickly and efficiently, by means of what are called **block moves.** In WordStar, most of the commands concerned with block moves are found in the second column of the ^K menu.

```
|   -Block Operations-   |
| B  Begin   K  End      |
| H  Hide/Display        |
| C  Copy    Y  Delete   |
| V  Move    W  Write    |
| N  Column now OFF      |
```

The Second Column of the ^K Menu

Marking Blocks

A **block** of text can be anything from fifty pages to one character—whatever you want. First, you mark where the block begins, by moving the cursor there and hitting **^KB.** **<B>** appears on the screen to mark that spot (for start of "Block"). Then you move the cursor to where you want the block to end, and hit **^KK.** This makes the whole block show up in reverse video (i.e. dark letters on a light background, instead of vice versa).

You can also mark blocks using function keys. If you're using WordStar Version 3.3 or later, the function-key guide at the bottom of the screen tells you which keys to use—**F7** ("begblk") to mark the beginning of a block, and **F8** ("endblk") to mark the end.

You can ^KB or ^KK in the middle of a line, or even in the middle of a word. If you want to move a whole paragraph intact, be sure to ^KK at the beginning of the first line after the paragraph, rather than at the end of the last line of the paragraph. In fact, this is a good rule for moving any "complete" line. When you don't want the line to run together with another line at its new location, include the carriage return at the end of the line when you mark the block.

Moving Blocks

Having marked the block, you now move the cursor to where you want to put the block (which also can be in the middle of a line) and hit **^KV.** That's all there is to it.

You might want to reform the text (^B) at the point where the block came from, as well as at its new home. If the block you moved wasn't a complete paragraph, there may be too many or too few spaces on one or both ends of it, in both its old and new locations. You can clean them up with a few editing commands.

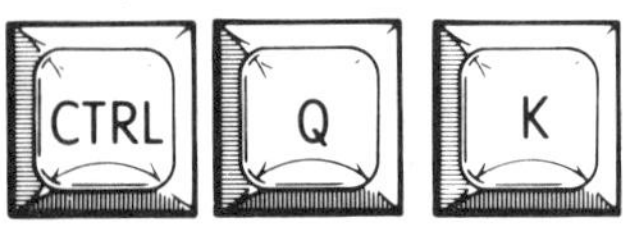

After moving a block, the cursor is at the new location. To get back to where you moved the block from, hit **^QV.** You can also move quickly to one end or the other of a marked block with **^QB** (which takes you to the beginning) and **^QK** (which takes you to the end). Obviously, ^QB and ^QK are of the most use when you're dealing with a large block of text.

The block remains in reverse video after the move. Any place markers—<1> to <9>—that were in the block do not move with it. They stay where the block used to be. If you don't plan to move a block again, you'll probably want to hide the block markers after the move, to prevent moving or deleting it accidentally. (I'll tell you how later.)

You can only mark one block at a time. If you try to ^KB or ^KK when you already have a <B> or <K> marked, the new marker will eliminate the old one.

Copying Blocks

It's also possible to move a block of text and still leave it where it was—that is, to copy it and put the copy in a new location. You do this just as above, except you hit ^**KC** instead of ^KV at the new location. You can put the same block of text in any number of different places just by moving the cursor to each place and hitting ^KC. The most recent copy is dimmed or in reverse video.

^KC will copy a block to a new location only in the same file. There are two other commands that let you copy blocks from one file to another: ^KW and ^KR.

^**KW** lets you extract a block of text from the file you're working on and save it as a separate file, so you can use it later in some other context. First you mark the block just as you would if you were going to copy it within the same file. Then hit ^KW and WordStar asks you:

NAME OF FILE TO WRITE MARKED TEXT ON?

This means: "What do you want to call this new file?"

If you give a name that already exists (let's say it's CHAPTER1), WordStar responds with:

FILE A:CHAPTER1 EXISTS — OVERWRITE? (Y/N):

(The "A:" indicates that this file which already exists is on the disk in drive A; if you're working on drive B, it will say "B:".)

If you respond with a Y (y, ^Y), WordStar will go ahead and make the marked block into a file named CHAPTER1, thereby destroying whatever the old CHAPTER1 file contained. If you respond with any other character, WordStar will move the cursor back to the line above so you can type in a new file name.

If you change your mind in the middle of all this, ^U (as always) will interrupt the command and return you—once you add an Esc—back to the text.

^**KR** is also a very useful command. It asks you for the name of a file and inserts the whole file into the file you're editing, right where the cursor is. A typical use for ^KR would be if you have **boilerplate** (chunks of text that you use over and over again, word for word, in varying contexts). You make each piece of boilerplate a file of its own, and ^KR it into the text wherever you need it. You can do the same for dozens of separate pieces of boilerplate—as many as you can fit on the disk.

A good way to look at ^KR is as the opposite of ^KW—^KW takes a part of the file you're working on and makes it a separate file, and ^KR takes a separate file and makes it part of the file you're working on. By using both commands, you can copy a block in one file to a new location in a separate file.

How big a block of text you can move depends on the amount of RAM your system has. If you're using WordStar Version 3.2 on a system with 64K memory, you'll be limited to blocks of 900 characters (about 13 lines with WordStar's default margins).

Deleting Blocks

You can also delete a block of text (this is faster than ^Ying out each of the lines). You mark the block, as above, and then hit **^KY.** You can do this from anywhere in the file; you don't have to be near the block you're deleting. But if you want to go where the block used to be, you can, by hitting ^QV after you delete.

^KY is a very powerful, and therefore very dangerous, command. It can wipe out an entire file, if the entire file has been marked as a block (which is completely possible, since marking the whole file as a block and then ^KCing is a good way to duplicate text). To make sure ^KY uses its great power for good and not for evil, use ^KH.

Hiding Blocks

^KH hides the block markers, so that they're not visible on your screen, and also makes them inoperable. If you hit ^KY now, WordStar will give you an error message and leave the block alone. Hitting ^KH again makes the markers reappear. You can't delete the markers unless you delete the block or close the file, so usually you'll just want to hide them when you're done working with a block.

WordStar normally moves, copies, or deletes every line in its entirety between the beginning and end of the marked block. This is the ordinary, margin-to-margin mode.

Column Blocks

But it's also possible to move (copy, delete) just a column of text, and leave the rest of each line of which the column is a part. (You can also move two or more columns together.) This is called column mode. Examples of both ordinary and column blocks are shown below.

Ordinary Block
(block marked is in boldface)

COUNTRY	HOMICIDE RATE	SUICIDE RATE
United States	8.50	15.52
<B>**Italy**	**7.38**	**7.67**
Finland	**6.45**	**23.35**
France	**1.53**	**14.83**
Switzerland	**1.42**<K>	33.72
Sweden	1.01	19.74

Column Block
(block marked is in boldface)

COUNTRY	HOMICIDE RATE	SUICIDE RATE
United States	8.50	15.52
<B>**Italy**	**7.38**	7.67
Finland	**6.45**	23.35
France	**1.53**	14.83
Switzerland	**1.42**<K>	33.72
Sweden	1.01	19.74

^**KN** toggles you back and forth between ordinary and column mode, and indicates the present status on the ^K menu with the message:

N Column now **OFF**

or, if you're using WordStar Version 3.2, with the message

N Column on (**OFF**)

If you wanted to move just a column, you would hit ^KN, and the line would read:

N Column now **ON**

or with Version 3.2:

N Column off (**ON**)

7 *Global Searches and Substitutions*

ANY POWERFUL EDITOR lets you do something that no typewriter can—find a word or phrase everywhere it occurs in a document, and automatically change it to another word if you want. Because this search or substitution isn't restricted to the cursor position but can zip through your whole file in one fell swoop, it's called "global."

Searching

WordStar offers a simple procedure for global searches and substitutions. If you type **^QF**, WordStar will ask you:

```
FIND?
```

Type in the sequence of characters (up to 30) you want to find, and hit ↵. This sequence can be a word, a phrase, a number, a control character, a symbol, or gibberish, so I'll refer to it by its technical name—a **string.** The first string we'll search for will be a phrase—"peace of mind".

```
FIND? peace of mind
```

By the way, 30 characters is virtually always enough, because even if you're looking for a long phrase, you don't need to type it out in its entirety. In this case, for example, "FIND? peace of m" would almost certainly have the same result as "FIND? peace of mind", because it's very unlikely that "peace of m" would occur anywhere but in the phrase "peace of mind".

WordStar now asks you if you want any options, and tells you that if you don't know what the various options are, you can hit ? to get a list of them:

```
OPTIONS? (? FOR INFO)
```

For the moment, just hit ↵, which is the equivalent of saying "no options"; I'll discuss the options in a little while.

WordStar now searches through the file for the first occurrence of "peace of mind". It moves forward, starting from where the cursor was when you typed ^QF, and it continues searching until it either finds the string or it hits the end of the file. So if "peace of mind" occurs only before the cursor position, WordStar won't find it. If you want to look for a word everywhere in a file, ^QR the cursor to the beginning of the file before searching with ^QF.

If WordStar finds "peace of mind", it will put the cursor on the space (or character) right after it, and rewrite the screen to show it and the text that surrounds it. If WordStar can't find "peace of mind", it will display:

```
*** NOT FOUND: "peace of mind" *** Press ESCAPE Key
```

Esc will take you back to the main menu. (Here, unlike many other places, only the Esc key will do. The other keys get you nothing.) Once you have returned to the main menu, ^QV will return the cursor to where it was before the ^QF command.

Searching and Replacing

Changing one string to another works in much the same way. You hit **^QA** and WordStar first asks what string you want to change:

```
FIND?
```

Say the string you want to change is the word "persons". You type it in and hit ↵. WordStar now asks you what you want to replace it with:

```
FIND? persons REPLACE WITH?
```

Say you want to replace it with "people". WordStar now asks you if you want any options:

```
FIND? persons REPLACE WITH? people
OPTIONS? (? FOR INFO)
```

(If there's room, all three questions will appear on the same line.)

If you now hit ↵, WordStar will find the next occurrence of "persons", put the cursor on (or under) the "p", and flash it back and forth between that position and the upper right corner of the screen, where this question will appear:

```
REPLACE (Y/N):
```

This is to make sure you don't make a change by mistake.

If you respond with a Y (or y or ^Y), WordStar will make the change and revise what's on the screen to show it. If you hit any other key, WordStar won't make the change. In either case, the cursor will move to the space immediately following the string. If you now want to put the cursor back where it was before you made the substitution, ^QV will do it.

Repeating Search or Replace Commands

It would get pretty tedious to have to keep typing ^QF or ^QA, followed by the string you want to find or replace, over and over again. So ^**L** (for "Last command") lets you repeat the last find command, or the last replace command up to the point where the message "REPLACE (Y/N):" appears on the screen.

You can work your way through a file this way, hitting ^L to get yourself to the next occurrence, and Y to approve the change. If you don't want to make the change, just hit any key other than Y to get past the string and then ^L to get to the next occurrence.

The Number Option

But there are even easier ways to make changes in bulk, and that's one of the functions of the OPTIONS question I said I'd get back to. Type ^QF, ask WordStar to look for "a", hit ↵ and when the options question comes on, type 4 (followed by ↵). WordStar will put the cursor immediately after the fourth occurrence of the letter *a*.

Now hit ^QR, then ^QA, and ask WordStar to find "a" and replace it with "x". Type 4 again as an answer to the options question. WordStar will bring the cursor to each of the first four *a*'s in the file and ask you if you want to change each one. Try typing Y for the first two but N for the third. WordStar leaves the third *a* alone and moves you to the fourth one. (It doesn't have to be an N; any key but a Y (y, ^Y) will result in leaving the change undone.)

Using the **number option** can save you several keystrokes and quite a bit of time over the ^L method (although ^L may be easier if you're going to repeat the command only once or twice). You can use any number up to 65,535—which, for all practical purposes, equals infinity. When WordStar hits the last occurrence, it will put the NOT FOUND message on the screen and ask you to hit Esc. To escape from the command without going through all the occurrences of the string in the file, type ^U ("cancel command"), followed by Esc.

If you use a number greater than the number of times the string you're searching for occurs in the file, you'll get a NOT FOUND message. This works fine with ^QA (it just tells you when you've run out of strings to substitute for), but with ^QF WordStar simply gives you the NOT FOUND message without showing you any of the occurrences it found. When you hit Esc, you're back in the file with the cursor at the end. ^QV will take you back to the last occurrence or substitution.

Replacing Everywhere in a File

Sometimes you want to find and replace everywhere in a file, not just from the cursor forward. To do this, you type **G** (which stands for "globally") as an option with ^QA.

WordStar first moves the cursor to the beginning of the file. It takes the cursor to each occurrence and asks if you want to change it (Y/N). You get a NOT FOUND message only if there are *no* occurrences of the string you're looking for. (It makes no sense to use the G option with ^QF.)

Replacing without Approval

There's an even more powerful way to make changes—the **N** option. N replaces without asking for your approval. Used with G (WordStar understands it both ways—**NG** or **GN**), it makes the ordered change everywhere in the file without asking for your OK. If you use this command and suddenly see it creating havoc in your file, you can stop it with ^U.

Using G or GN as an option is the easiest way to make mass substitutions, unless you need to make other editing commands between the replacements. In that case it's best to ^QR to the start of the file, ^QA with no options, and ^L to repeat the command each time you're done editing.

To do mass substitutions as fast as possible, use the G (or a large number) option in conjunction with the N option. Even then, however, WordStar is slowed up by having to show you each change on the screen. You can speed up the process immensely by saving WordStar this trouble. Just hit any key while the command is executing (pick a harmless one, like the Spacebar). The cursor will stop where it was, and WordStar will make the substitutions without showing them to you.

Since hitting Spacebar (or some other key) during a global replace speeds up the process and hides what's being done, it's *not* the thing to do if you see something going wrong. Instead, hit ^U to interrupt the execution. Any other key is only going to make things worse for you.

If you want to insert the same string (phrase, etc.) over and over again at different places in a file, WordStar has a way to make that easy for you. Type ^QA and hit ⏎ (nothing else) when you're asked what you want to find. After the question REPLACE WITH? type the string you want to insert. Choose the N option. Now move the cursor to where you want the string inserted and hit ^L. Each time you do that, the string appears.

Repeating with Different Options

There's one additional way to save yourself tedious retyping when doing global searches and substitutions. It involves **^R** (for "repeat"). Let's say you want to repeat a find command, but with different options. You don't want to have to retype the string you're looking for. Hit ^QF and then ^R. The string will appear. You can modify it if you want (using the commands displayed in the two-line mini-menu directly above it), or just hit ⏎ to keep it as it is. Then you'll be asked what options you want, as usual.

This same method works with ^QA. ^R will bring back the last string searched for and the last string that replaced it; just type ^R, followed by ⏎, in answer to each question. And you can also use ^R to bring back the options you used last, whether you're finding or replacing. Of course, if you're not going to change any part of the command, ^L is an easier way to repeat it.

Mass Deletions

To delete a string, type ^QA and the string you want to delete after FIND?. Then hit ⏎ (nothing else) when you're asked what you want to replace it with. WordStar will find the next occurrence of the string and replace it with nothing—that is, delete it. You can use a G or GN option with this command to kill a string everywhere it occurs in a file.

One common use of such a mass deletion is to adapt a file that wasn't created by WordStar for use with WordStar. Often the problem with such a file is that each line of text ends with a "hard carriage return," which prevents WordStar from reforming them into paragraphs. Each line in such a file would be a paragraph of its own. So you want to kill all the carriage returns except the ones that are actually at the end of a paragraph.

To do that, type ^Q and ask WordStar to find ^N (which, as you may recall, is the command for inserting a hard carriage return). When asked what you want to replace it with, hit the ↵ key to indicate "nothing." Choose the N option, but not the G option, since you may want to do a little editing between certain of these deletions.

When you type the ↵ after the N, WordStar will find the first carriage return in the file and kill it. Type ^L to get the next, the next, and so on until you get to the end of the paragraph. Leave that last carriage return at the end of the paragraph and move the cursor back to the beginning of the paragraph. Now hit ^B and watch the paragraph reform.

Move the cursor to the beginning of the next paragraph (past the carriage return you left at the end of the first paragraph) and repeat the process.

Searching Backwards

Typing a **B** after the option question will make WordStar search backward through the file, rather than forward. It's easier to do this than to ^QR if you're at the end of the file, and of course it's also useful for finding the last (or last couple of) occurrences of a string, rather than the next, or the first.

Searching for Whole Words Only

It's very important when doing global finds and substitutions to remember how literal-minded a computer is. For example, if you ask WordStar to search for "the", it will find not only occurrences of the English word "the" but also any other place where those three letters appear as part of another word—as in "them", "there", "lathe", and "fathead". To get WordStar to look only for the English word "the", you have to ask it to find " the "—or specify the **W** option.

With the W option, WordStar finds only whole words—that is, occurrences of the string you're looking for that have no letters (or numbers) before or after them. This is more accurate than leaving a space on either side of the word, because it also allows for punctuation marks. So, if you ask WordStar to find "the" with the W option, it will skip over "then" and "lathe" and "fathead" but find " the ",

"(the ", "—the ", etc. (It would also find " the.", " the?", and " the!" if, for some strange reason, you had the word "the" at the end of a sentence.)

The W option has one limitation—it can't find a word at the very beginning or end of a file. There must be at least one character or space before and after the word.

Ignoring Upper- and Lowercase

The literalness of computers also applies to capital and lowercase letters. If you search for "the", you won't find occurrences of "The"; likewise, "The" won't turn up occurrences of "the"—*unless* you specify **U** as an option (for "ignore uppercase"). With the U option, the distinction between caps and lowercase letters is ignored—so, for example, searching for "us" with the U option would turn up "us", "Usually", "US policy", and "GnuStar" (you think it's easy to find an example of a small *u* followed by a capital *S*?).

Options can be combined, and the order doesn't matter. So, for example, you could search for "or" and specify 5BUW as your options. WordStar would find the fifth occurrence before the cursor position of "or", "OR", "Or", or "oR" and would ignore those two letters when they occurred in the middle of another word.

The Options Menu

To refresh your memory of all the options available to you while in the middle of typing a ^QF or ^QA command, type **?** in response to the OPTIONS question, and WordStar will display a small reminder menu. You can move on from this menu just by typing the option(s) that you want—followed by ↵, or simply ↵ if you don't want any options. And you can skip the whole options question just by hitting Esc instead of ↵ right before the question normally appears (that is, after answering the question FIND? if you're ^QFing or after answering the question REPLACE WITH? if you're ^QAing).

There are other, even fancier features of WordStar's global find and replace function, but they're too obscure for an introductory book like this.

8 *File Handling*

SOME OF THE MORE BASIC file handling commands have already been covered: ^KD, ^KX, ^KS and ^KQ, which save or abandon the file you're working on (see Chapter 4); ^KR, which inserts another file into the one you're editing; and ^KW, which does just the opposite—that is, takes a chunk of the file you're working on and makes a new, separate file of it (see Chapter 6).

In this chapter, I'll explain the other file handling capabilities and considerations. The easiest way to begin doing this is to discuss each of the commands listed on the opening menu.

```
not editing
            < < <   O P E N I N G   M E N U   > > >
- - -Preliminary Commands- - - | - -File Commands- - | -System Commands-
L Change logged disk drive     |                     | R Run a program
F File directory now ON        | P Print a file      | X EXIT to system
H Set help level               |                     |
- - -Commands to Open a file- - -|                   | -WordStar Options-
  D Open a document file       | E RENAME a file     | T Run TelMerge
  N Open a non-document file   | O COPY a file       | M Run MailMerge
                               | Y DELETE a file     | S Run SpellStar
DIRECTORY of disk A:
PRINT.TST   WS.COM   WSMSGS.OVR   WSOVLY1.OVR
```

The Opening Menu

Changing the Logged Disk

The first column of the opening menu lists several "preliminary commands"—things you do before editing or file handling. The first of these, **L,** is very straightforward. If you want to:

1. work on another disk;
2. go to the other drive to see what files are on the disk in it; or
3. just see which drive you're logged onto;

hit L. (You don't need to follow it with a ↵.) The L command display appears.

```
L              not editing

  The LOGGED DISK (or Current Disk or Default Disk) is the
  disk drive used for files except those files for which
  you enter a disk drive name as part of the file name.
  WordStar displays the File Directory of the Logged Disk.

  THE LOGGED DISK DRIVE IS NOW A:

  NEW LOGGED DISK DRIVE (letter, colon, RETURN)? ▲

DIRECTORY of disk A:
 PRINT.TST          WS.COM      WSMSGS.OVR     WSOVLY1.OVR
```

The L Command Display

To log onto another drive, type A or B (or C or D) and then ↵ (you don't need the colon). To leave the logged drive unchanged, hit ^U or ↵. To return to the opening menu from the L command display, or from any other command display, hit Esc.

You can also change the logged drive while editing, without having to go through the opening menu, by hitting **^KL.**

Listing File Names

Hitting **F** under the opening menu turns off the directory of files at the bottom of the opening menu and the command displays, and changes the F line on the opening menu to read:

F File directory now **OFF**–

The file directory is now off; hitting F will turn it on again. If you're using WordStar version 3.2, the menu reads

F = File directory on (**OFF**)

This message won't win any prizes for syntax, but it means the same thing.

If you put a new disk in the logged drive, the directory will continue to show the files on the previous disk, until you either:

- hit L, followed by the name of the logged drive (so if you're logged onto A, you'd type L, A, ⟵); or
- type F twice in a row.

If you want the directory of files on the disk to be displayed while you're actually editing (and not just below the opening menu), use ^**KF**. The directory will appear between the last line of the menu and the ruler line. To turn the directory display off, hit ^KF again. Sometimes WordStar will display only part of a long directory; you can get the rest with ^Z and ^W.

Getting On-Screen Help

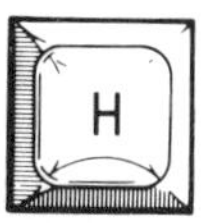

Hitting **H** under the opening menu takes you to the same help menu that hitting ^JH does when you are editing under the main menu. Key F1, however, will take you to the help menu from either menu and is probably simpler to use. All the options and commands are the same regardless of where you come to the help menu from (although you return to different places afterwards). For details on what they are, see the discussion of the help menu towards the end of Chapter 5.

Opening Files

The next section covers the opening of files. You're already acquainted with the D command display and the enormous variety of activities that flow from it. **N** is similar to D; their command displays are virtually identical.

```
N               not editing

   Use this command to create and alter program source files
     and other non-documents. Word wrap defaults off;
     tabbing defaults to fixed (TAB chars in file; 8-col stops);
     page breaks not shown; hi bit flags not used in file.
   For normal word processing uses, use the "D" command instead.

       A file name is 1-8 letters/digits, a period,
       and an optional 1-3 character type.
       File name may be preceded by a disk drive letter A-D
       and colon, otherwise current logged disk is used.

       NAME OF FILE TO EDIT? ▲

partial DIRECTORY of disk A:      ^Z=scroll up
  PRINT.TST           WS.COM      WSMSGS.OVR     WSOVLY1.OVR
```

The N Command Display

Non-Document Files

But the file you open under N is a **non-document file.** Non-document files have the advantage of being compatible with programs other than WordStar. WordStar assures their compatibility by handling them differently from regular files, in the following ways:

1. Automatic page break calculation doesn't work. Page break display can't be turned on.
2. Word wrap, right justification, variable tabbing and display of the ruler line come turned off. But, unlike page break display, you can turn them on if you want (although this may destroy the file's compatibility).
3. Dot commands (which are covered in Chapter 10) aren't checked during editing. Therefore, no ?s appear at the end of a line that has a dot (period) in the first column.

4. Instead of showing you what page and what line of that page you're on, the status line shows you how many characters and how many lines are in the file from the beginning up to the cursor.

The middle column of the opening menu deals with file handling proper. The first command, P, is used to print out files. This subject is covered in detail in Chapter 11.

Renaming Files

The next command, **E,** is used to rename files. When you hit an E under the opening menu, the **E** command display appears.

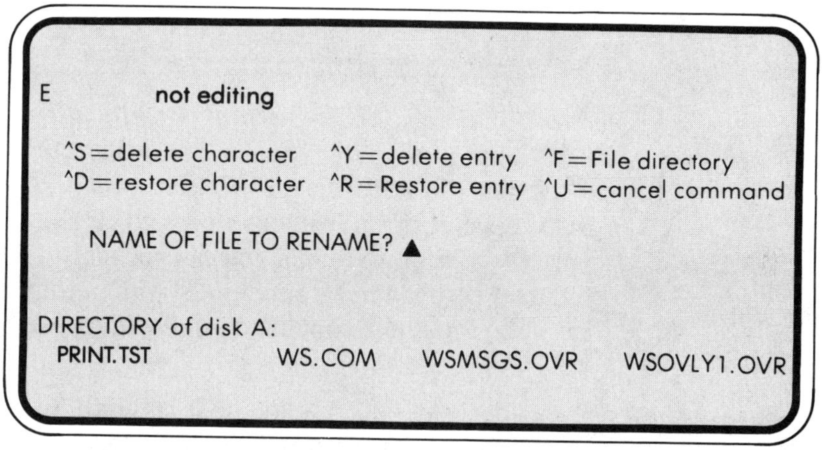

The E Command Display

You just type in the name of the file you want to rename, and hit ↵. If you want to rename a file on a drive other than the one you're logged onto, put the name of the drive the file is on, followed by a colon, in front of the file name. WordStar then asks you:

NEW NAME?

You type in what you want the new name for the file to be, hit ↵, and it's done. With **^KE,** you can get to the E command display while you're editing.

Deleting Files

Let's skip down to the bottom and cover the **Y** command. Use Y when you want to delete a file. It gives you this command display:

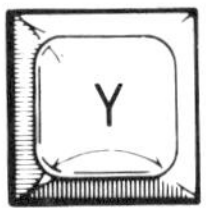


```
Y            not editing

  ^S=delete character    ^Y=delete entry    ^F=File directory
  ^D=restore character   ^R=Restore entry   ^U=cancel command

     NAME OF FILE TO DELETE? ▲

DIRECTORY of disk A:
  PRINT.TST          WS.COM     WSMSGS.OVR     WSOVLY1.OVR
```

The Y Command Display

You just type in the name of the file you want deleted, and follow it with ⟵┘. After the file is deleted, you're returned automatically to the opening menu (without having to hit Esc). If you decide not to kill a file after you've hit Y, you can get back to the opening menu by hitting ^U followed by Esc, or ⟵┘ with nothing in front of it. (You can also get to the Y command display when you're editing, by typing **^KJ**.)

Copying Files

The last "file command" is **O**, which lets you copy files without having to use PC DOS's COPY command. When you hit O, the following command display appears:

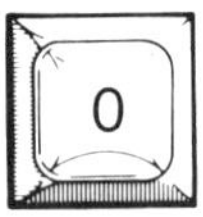


```
O            not editing

  ^S=delete character    ^Y=delete entry    ^F=File directory
  ^D=restore character   ^R=Restore entry   ^U=cancel command

     NAME OF FILE TO COPY FROM? ▲

DIRECTORY of disk A:
  PRINT.TST          WS.COM     WSMSGS.OVR     WSOVLY1.OVR
```

The O Command Display

The line that says:

NAME OF FILE TO COPY FROM?

means "Which file do you want to make a copy of?" The line that says:

NAME OF FILE TO COPY TO?

means "What do you want the copy to be called?"

You can specify which disk the file you're copying is on, and/or which disk you want the copy put on, by adding the name of a drive and a colon in front of either file name. You don't *have* to specify the drive; WordStar will just assume the logged drive for both.

If you try to give the copy a name that's already being used for some other file, you get a message that reads:

FILE [name you tried to use] EXISTS — OVERWRITE? (Y/N):

If you do want to overwrite the existing file (i.e., substitute this new one for it), hit Y for yes. This will destroy the existing file, make the copy as requested, and give the copy the destroyed file's name.

If you've made a mistake and don't want to overwrite the file, hit any key other than Y. The NAME OF FILE TO COPY TO? question will be repeated, so you can think up a new name to call the copy. If you've changed your mind about the whole thing, ⟵ by itself, or ^U followed by Esc, will return you to the opening menu. (^**KO** will get you to the O command display while editing.)

Running Other Programs

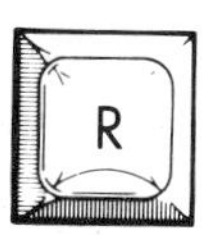

The last column begins with two "system commands." **R** is used to run a program other than WordStar without having to exit from WordStar. Most often this is PCDOS's CHKDSK program, which tells you how much space is available on a disk, but it can be any program (i.e., "executable" file) that's on the disk.

The R command display looks like this:

```
R          not editing

 Enter name of program you wish to Run,
 optionally followed by appropriate arguments.
   Example (shows disk space):     STAT

 ^S=delete character   ^Y=delete entry   ^F=File directory
 ^D=restore character  ^R=Restore entry  ^U=cancel command

   COMMAND? ▲

DIRECTORY of disk A:
  PRINT.TST          WS.COM      WSMSGS.OVR      WSOVLY1.OVR
```

The R Command Display

"COMMAND?" means "What program do you want to run?" "Arguments" is computer jargon for extra specifications you want to add to the command or program.

You just type in the name of the program and hit ↵. Although the program name includes the extension .COM, do not type it in. When you're done with the program you've run, you can return to WordStar by hitting any key.

Make sure you only try to run programs that are executable. If you try to run a file that isn't executable, you'll get an error message if you're lucky. If you're not, you'll get a locked keyboard; no key will do anything, and you'll be forced to reboot, losing any text you haven't saved.

As a general rule, R will not run a PC DOS program if there is a WordStar command that will do the same thing (for example, save, copy, delete, or rename files). One exception to this is the PC DOS command DIR which lists the files on the disk along with the size of each. DIR will not run under WordStar, even though the comparable WordStar commands (F and ^KF) give only the file names and not their sizes. So to find out the size of each file, you'll have to exit WordStar and then run DIR.

You can't get directly to the R command display while editing. If you want to run another program and then return to the file you're editing, you have to save the file you're working on, return to the opening menu, go to the R command display, run the program, go back to the opening menu, and then back to editing through D.

Exiting WordStar

The last system command is **X,** which takes you out of WordStar and puts you back in the operating system. As was mentioned in Chapter 4, ^KX from the main menu will do the same thing, stopping first to save the file you're working on.

If you have purchased MicroPro's optional programs MailMerge, SpellStar, or TelMerge, you can run them from the opening menu. M calls up MailMerge, which is the subject of Chapter 12. S calls up SpellStar, which is the subject of Chapter 13. T calls up TelMerge, a program for communicating with other computers. (Depending on your version of WordStar, TelMerge may not appear on the opening menu.)

That covers the commands found on the opening menu, but there are a few more things to say about file handling, and how WordStar works in general.

A Shortcut

There's a quicker way to begin editing than typing ws(↵) to get to the opening menu, D to get to the D command display and then the name of the file you want to work on followed by ↵ to get to the main menu. Instead, you can just type the filename directly after ws, and follow it with a ↵:

```
A>ws chapter1.doc ↵
```

This loads both WordStar and the file (assuming they are both in drive A) and takes you directly to the main menu.

Interrupting Commands

Remember that ^U will interrupt the execution of just about anything. If there was something to interrupt, the screen will show:

```
*** INTERRUPTED ***
```

and you'll have to press Esc to get back to where you were. If nothing is interrupted, ^U will return you to where you were immediately.

Long Files

Because WordStar moves portions of the workfile back and forth between the disk and RAM, instead of keeping it all in RAM, you can work with **very long files** if you need to. You might want a long file because, unless you have MailMerge (covered in Chapter 12), WordStar requires that:

1. a page break must occur between the printout of any two files;
2. automatic page numbering must be reset for each file being printed out;
3. you have to give a new print command for each file being printed out—that is, you can't link them.

However, unless you need long files because of these requirements, it's better to keep your files of moderate size (one-third of the capacity of your work disk at most).

One reason is that many WordStar commands execute more slowly in long files. Another reason is that large files create a risk of losing data, because they can make for **full disks** when you save them.

As I explained in Chapter 4, when WordStar saves a file, it takes what's in memory and writes it to the disk using the .$$$ type for a temporary file. When the new version has been correctly written to the disk, it replaces .$$$ with the type you gave it, renames the older version of the disk .BAK, and erases the old back-up file.

In order for WordStar to carry out these steps, there has to be enough room on the disk for three entire copies of the file. Logically then, a file can't take up more than one third of the disk (even assuming you have only that file on the disk). If WordStar tries to save the file and there's not enough room for all three, it automatically changes its procedure and erases the old back-up file first to make room on the disk for the new version. (It puts a warning message on the screen to tell you it's doing this.)

If there's not enough room on the disk for even two copies of the file, WordStar will refuse to finish saving the file. On the screen you'll see

```
*** ERROR E12: DISK FULL *** Press ESCAPE Key
```

Recovering from Disk-Full Problems

After hitting Esc, first try to delete any unnecessary files from the disk with ^KJ. You can also delete any file you know you'll be able to replace later (by copying it from another disk). Even WS.COM or WSMSGS.OVR can be deleted if necessary (since you're sure to have them on other disks). If that doesn't do it, there are several other things you can try:

1. If you haven't made many changes since the last save, it might be easiest to just abandon the file (i.e., exit WordStar without saving), make more room on the disk (or copy the file to a disk with more room), and start again.
2. If there's extra space on the disk in the other drive, try putting part of the file (the part you've made changes in) onto that disk, with ^KW. You can later recombine that new file with the rest of the file you're editing on a disk with more space.
3. You can delete parts of the file that you haven't changed until the file is short enough to save without getting a disk-full error. Then you can retrieve the deleted parts from a backup file. (This maneuver is a lot safer to do if you have a backup of the file on a separate disk.)
4. If none of those techniques works, here's a desperation move. Don't use it unless your only alternative is to lose a whole lot of work by not saving. First, ^QC to see if the cursor can move to the end of the file. (If it can't, there's no hope.) Then, use ^KJ to delete the file you're working on from the disk (that is, delete the file your workfile is a copy of). Then save.

WordStar may crash with fatal error F29. A **fatal error** is one that terminates the program. The results of fatal errors vary: a locked-up keyboard, garbage or some bizarre repetitive pattern on the screen, or a sudden return to the operating system. But the net effect is the same—the program is dead and all the work you did since the last save is gone.

In this particular case, however, don't let the fatal error message phase you. Your file will have the type .$$$; use E from the opening menu to rename it .DOC or .TXT or whatever. There will be no backup file. Clear sufficient space on another disk and make a backup.

Sometimes you get a second disk-full error message when you hit Esc (and a third and a fourth if you keep hitting it). This means you're completely out of luck. Your disk is *really* full and the file you were editing is irretrievable. The only way around this one—and the best way around all disk-full errors—is to watch your disk space. Prevent disk-full errors by keeping plenty of extra space on your disks.

If you *have* to have a huge file, there's one other thing you can do—you can instruct WordStar to switch drives every time it saves the file. You do this when entering WordStar by typing:

```
A>ws a:article.doc b:(↵)
```

Make sure you don't type anything after the "b:", not even a space. (If A is the logged drive, you can omit it; i.e., the line would read, "A>ws article.doc b:".) WordStar will now save the file on the disk in drive B, calling it ARTICLE.DOC, and rename the file on the disk in drive A (i.e., the file you started out with) ARTICLE.BAK.

If you ^KS and continue to edit, then the next time you save, the new file will be put on drive A (overwriting the original), and the first save (on drive B) will be renamed ARTICLE.BAK. Saves will continue to alternate between drives. This method lets you work with files that are as large as the capacity of the disk (minus the 78K or so that WordStar itself takes up)—assuming you have some compelling need to. If you don't, remember: *The easiest way to avoid all these problems is simply not to work with long files in the first place.*

You can find out how long a file is in several ways:

1. From the operating system (use ^KX to get there if you're editing), type DIR and press ↵ to list each file and its size.
2. Hit ^QC and ^OP (in either order). This gives you the size of the file in characters and lines, but no information about other files on the disk.
3. There's also an indirect indication. When ^QR (which

moves the cursor to the beginning of the file) takes a couple of seconds to execute, the file is probably still small enough to be held entirely in RAM. When ^QR starts taking minutes, the file is large.

To keep a file small by splitting it, mark a large hunk, starting at the beginning, as a block. Then ^KW the block as a separate file, and delete the block from the first file. You can do this several times if necessary. Call the first block you save as a file LETTERA (or CHAP3A, or whatever), the second LETTERB (CHAP3B), etc. After you're done editing the last part and have saved it, rename it LETTERC (or whatever).

If you're using a version of WordStar earlier than 3.3, or working on a computer that has less than 128K of RAM, DISK FULL problems may also be caused simply by moving around in long files. Some suggestions for dealing with these problems are in Appendix E, "Special Note for Earlier Versions of WordStar."

9 On-Screen Formatting

MOST WORD PROCESSING SYSTEMS do their formatting during printout, and leave the text on the screen the way you entered it. WordStar, however, lets you see the effect of most formatting changes on the screen, so you can evaluate them immediately.

The ^O menu controls **on-screen formatting** (O for "on-screen," of course). It looks like this:

```
^O   A:PRACTICE.DOC    PAGE 1   LINE 1   COL 01           INSERT ON

              < < <      O N S C R E E N   M E N U      > > >

-Margins & Tabs-   |   -Line Functions-    |   - -More Toggles- -      |   -Other Menus-
L Set left margin  | C Center text         | J Justify       now ON    |  (from Main only)
R Set right margin | S Set line spacing    | V Vari-tabs     now ON    | ^J Help    ^K Block
X Release margins  |                       | H Hyph-help     now ON    | ^Q Quick   ^P Print
I Set   N Clear tab|    - - -Toggles- - -  | E Soft hyph     now OFF   | ^O Onscreen
G Paragraph tab    | W Wrd wrap now ON     | D Prnt disp     now ON    | Space bar returns
F Ruler from line  | T Rlr line now ON     | P Pge break     now ON    | you to Main Menu.

L- - - -!- - - -!- - - -!- - - -!- - - -!- - - -!- - - -!- - - -!- - - -!- - - - - - - - -R
```

The ^O Menu

Setting the Margins

In the first column are the commands that control margins and tabs. **^OL** sets the left margin. (You can also use the function key **F3.**) When you type that command, the question:

LEFT MARGIN COLUMN NUMBER (ESCAPE for cursor column)?

appears on the screen. You answer the question with the number of the column you want the first letters of full lines to appear in (that is, the first space to the right of the left margin). If the cursor is in that column, hit Esc and WordStar will automatically enter that number for you. (The number of the column the cursor is in is indicated in the status line at the top of the screen.)

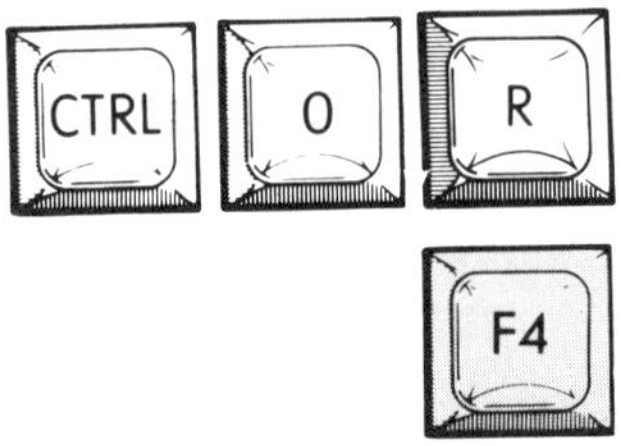

^OR (or its equivalent, **F4**) works in just the same way for the right margin—you indicate what you want to be the last column of text (that is, the last space before the right margin). Esc automatically inputs the column the cursor is in. After changing the margins, use ^B to see how your text looks with new margins.

^OX releases the margins—you can move the cursor beyond them and insert text. When you bring the cursor back within the margins, the margin release turns off and you won't be able to move the cursor outside the margins, unless you type ^OX again.

If you type ^OX and change your mind, you can turn it off without having to move the cursor beyond the margins, just by typing ^OX. In other words, ^OX is a toggle (on/off switch).

When the margins are released, the words MAR REL appear in the status line. Basically, ^OX has the effect of turning word wrap off until the cursor has gone beyond the margins and come back between them.

Setting the Tabs

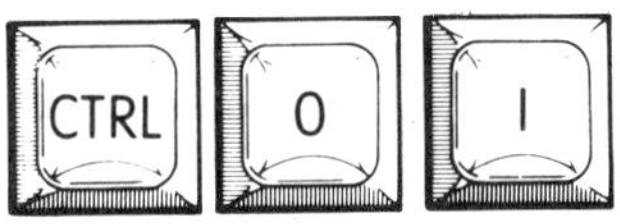

^OI is used to set tab stops. When you type it, the question:

SET TAB AT COLUMN (ESCAPE for cursor column)?

appears on the screen. You answer with the number of the column where you want to set a tab. An **!** appears on the ruler line to show where the new tab stop is. As with the margin-setting commands, hitting Esc indicates that you want a tab at the column that the cursor is in. **^O(⇆)**, substituting the tab key for the letter *i*, has the same effect as **^OI.**

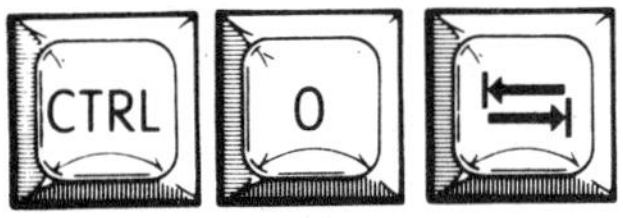

Above the words SET TAB AT COLUMN, another line of text appears, which reads:

For decimal tab stop enter # and decimal point column

This message appears because WordStar lets you enter two kinds of tabs—normal and decimal. With normal tabs (each shown as an ! on the ruler line) the first letters or numbers of all the entries in a column line up. With decimal tabs, WordStar automatically lines up all the decimal points instead. If you ever deal with columns of numbers, decimal tabs are a godsend. You can go nuts trying to line up the numbers otherwise.

To ask for a decimal tab, insert the symbol # in front of the column number. A # will appear on the ruler line to indicate where the decimal tab is. When you tab to a column that's set for a decimal tab, the word "decimal" appears on the status line to remind you that text will be lined up in terms of decimal points. (If you move to that column in some other way, this doesn't happen.)

Hitting ⇆ takes you to ! and # tabs indiscriminately, but once you start entering text, WordStar remembers which is which and moves the text around accordingly.

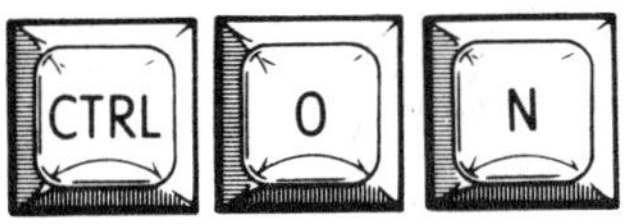

^**ON** clears tab stops. When you hit it, the question:

CLEAR TAB AT COL (ESCAPE for cursor col; A for all)?

appears on the screen. You answer with the number of the column where you want to remove a tab stop. If you want to clear all the tab stops, type A.

Setting a Temporary Left Margin

Sometimes you want to indent every line of a paragraph, not just the first (as when you're typing an outline). WordStar makes this easy. ^**OG** (or its equivalent, **F2**) makes all the lines of a paragraph start at the first tab stop, instead of at the left margin. Hitting ^OG again makes them start at the second tab stop, and so on. This lasts only until you:

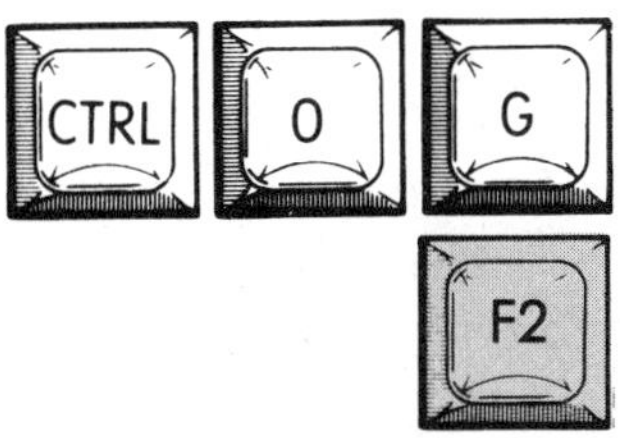

1. hit ↵ (as you do to indicate the end of a paragraph);
2. change the margins; or
3. move the cursor to any point in the text above where it was when you typed ^OG.

WordStar lets you know that ^OG is in effect by highlighting (or reversing) the ruler line up to the first tab (or second or third tab, if you've ^OGed more than once). But even without highlighting or reverse video, it's pretty obvious, because all the text you enter starts five (or however many) spaces from the left margin.

Making Your Own Ruler Line

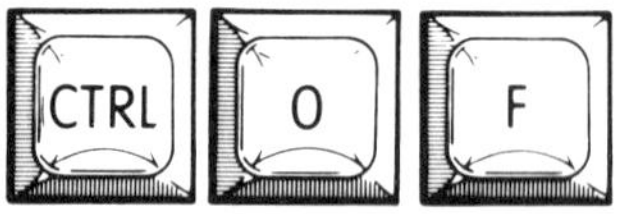

WordStar offers you yet another way to set tabs— **^OF.** This command makes it easy to reset all the tabs and both margins in one fell swoop. It's used mostly for tables, or anywhere you have a special format that's different from the one you use for the rest of the text. ^OF really starts to pay off when you want to use it several times for similar tables or other special pieces of text. It involves creating a substitute ruler line, and here's how you do it.

Put the cursor at the beginning of the first line of the table (or other piece of text) that you want formatted in the new way. Hit ^N to give yourself a new blank line to work on. Then type two periods (. .), ^P and ↵. (This causes WordStar to treat the line as a "comment" and therefore ignore it when printing out the file.)

Now move the cursor over to where you want the left margin to be, and start typing hyphens (-). (Make sure that the line "E Soft hyph now" in the third column of the ^O menu reads "**OFF**" before typing the line.) Put a ! everywhere you want a regular tab stop, a # everywhere you want a decimal tab stop, and hyphens everywhere else. End the line with ↵ where you want the right margin to be.

To activate this line, put the cursor anywhere on it and type ^OF. This substitute ruler line will now become the real ruler line. The old margins and tabs will be cleared, and the ones you've indicated in your ruler line will be substituted for them. Try it.

If you're going to use this format line more than once, it probably makes sense to create another one containing the normal text parameters (the ones you just switched away from). Then you can toggle back and forth between them—text, table, text, and so on.

Centering Lines

The second column of the ^O menu begins with the commands for centering lines and changing line spacing. To center a line between the margins, put the cursor anywhere on it and type **^OC.** WordStar will center the characters in the line, ignoring spaces at either end of it.

Spacing Lines

WordStar lets you change the line spacing from single to double to triple or more. You type ^**OS** and the words:

ENTER space OR NEW LINE SPACING (1-9):

appear on the screen. An answer of 2 will get you doublespacing; an answer of 3, triplespacing; and right on up to 9, which will put 8 blanks lines between every line of text. (WordStar never leaves a feature out just because you're unlikely to need it.) To change the line spacing in text you've already entered, you'll need to use ^B as well.

The rest of the second column of the ^O menu, and all of the third column, relate to formatting functions that you can turn on and off (toggles). After each command, WordStar tells you if the function controlled by it is "now ON" or "now OFF". In version 3.2, the menu instead shows "on(OFF)" or "off(ON)".

Turning Word-Wrap Off

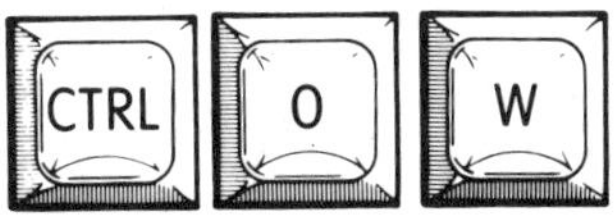

^**OW**, which controls word wrap, is the first toggle listed. Word wrap comes turned on, since that's the normal way of working in WordStar. With word wrap on, as you know, you don't have to type ↵ at the end of each line (in fact, you shouldn't). Instead, you just keep typing and when a word won't fit on the line you're on, WordStar moves the whole word down to the next line and starts a new line for you automatically.

With word wrap off, you have to decide for yourself where to end each line, using ↵. Turning word wrap off is useful for text you want formatted just the way you type it, like a table.

Hiding the Ruler Line

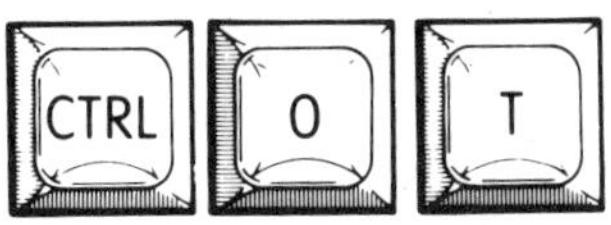

^**OT** turns the ruler line off, in case you don't like looking at it. Even when it's invisible, the ruler line is still in effect; that is, the margins and tabs that are set on it still apply. ^OT just controls the *display* of the ruler line. In normal operation, of course, the ruler line shows so you can see where your margins and tabs are, and thus the default for ^OT is ON.

Justifying the Right Margin

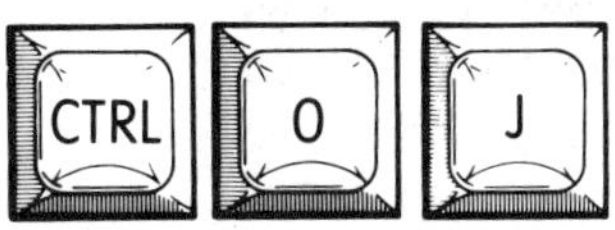

^**OJ** controls justification of the right margin. With ^OJ on (which is the default), each line is padded with spaces (between words on the screen and, on some printers, between letters and words during printout) so that the last letter of each line is at the right margin. This makes the right edge of the text straight, as it typically is in typeset material. (The left edge of the text is always straight.)

Spaces inserted by WordStar to justify a line are called **soft spaces,** because they come and go when words are added or deleted from the line, when the margins are changed, etc. They're different from **hard spaces,** which are are inserted by you and remain in the text regardless of how it's reformed.

With right justification off, these soft spaces aren't added and those that have previously been inserted will be removed when you reformat with ^B. This gives you a "ragged right" margin, which is typical of typed material.

Turning Variable Tabs Off

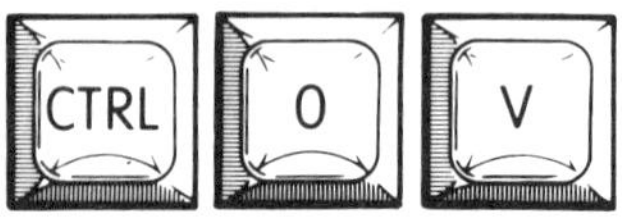

^OV turns the variable tab feature on and off. When variable tabs are on (the default), the tab stops shown on the ruler line are in effect. With ^OV off, tab stops are non-variable, and are set every 8 spaces. The ruler line will still show the variable tabs, but they won't work.

Hyphenation

^OH turns **hyphen help** on and off. And what, you ask, is "hyphen help"? Hyphen help is one of WordStar's jazzier features.

When you ^B to reform a paragraph with hyphen help on (and it's on until you turn it off), WordStar will find any long words that almost fit at the end of a line, but which had to be moved down to the next line, leaving a big gap. Then it will check to see if the word contains two or more syllables (don't ask me how it does that). *Then* it will figure out, more or less, where the word should be hyphenated, put the cursor there, and stop so you can decide if you want to hyphenate the word or not.

The following message will appear at the top of the screen:

TO HYPHENATE, PRESS –. Before pressing –, you may
move cursor: ^S = cursor left, ^D = cursor right.
If hyphenation not desired, type ^B.

This is all pretty self-explanatory. If the cursor is in the right place to split the word, and you want to hyphenate it, you just hit the hyphen (-) key. By the way, don't confuse hyphens with **dashes.** Hyphens separate parts of words, or parts of compound words; dashes, which are longer, separate phrases and clauses. A hyphen looks like this in typeset text: - ; a dash in typeset text looks like this: —, and like this in typescript: --.

If the cursor isn't in exactly the right place to split the word (what do you expect of a computer anyway?), move it to the right place (using arrow keys) and then hit the hyphen key. You can use other commands (like ^Z) too. But if you move the cursor out of the word, or if you enter any character other than a hyphen, the hyphen message will clear and you'll be out of hyphen help for that particular word.

The hyphens inserted by hyphen help are **soft hyphens** (similar to soft spaces and soft carriage returns). If you later reform so that the hyphenated word doesn't fall over the end of a line, the soft hyphen will disappear. But it will reappear in the same spot if the word ever falls over the end of a line again.

You can also insert **hard hyphens,** of course, as you would want to do in words that are always hyphenated regardless of where they fall, like higgledy-piggledy or tic-tac-toe. If for some reason you decide you want to enter a hard hyphen instead of a soft hyphen when the hyphen message is on the screen, hit ^P- instead of -.

If you don't want to hyphenate the word the cursor has stopped at, hit ^B, and reforming will continue. Hyphen help may stop you several times during the reforming of a paragraph. If you know in advance that you're not going to want to hyphenate any words at the end of lines, turn hyphen help off with the ^OH toggle.

Sometimes, of course, hyphen help doesn't stop ^B at all. This usually means that there are no long words in the paragraph that have to be pushed to the start of a new line. But it can also happen when there are long words if WordStar thinks they have only one syllable, or if WordStar thinks that even the first syllable won't fit at the end of the line.

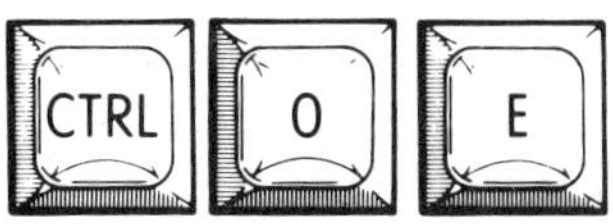

Because your judgment is (hopefully) more sophisticated than a mere computer program's, WordStar lets you insert soft hyphens on your own, without having to be asked by hyphen help if you want to do that. That's what the next toggle, **^OE,** is for.

^OE is the only one of the formatting toggles that comes turned off. With it off, typing a hyphen produces a hard hyphen—that is, one that will print out anywhere. With ^OE on, typing a hyphen produces a soft hyphen—that is, one that will only print out when the word it's in falls across the right margin.

Soft hyphens are always inserted into the text (rather than written over an existing character), whether ^V (insertion mode) is on or off. They look just like hard hyphens on the screen, unless you have highlighting, in which case they appear dimmer, or in reverse video.

If you make changes in the text, you need to reform it with ^B to get the soft hyphens to print out correctly. If you don't ^B after making changes, some soft hyphens may appear in the printout where they shouldn't, and some may fail to appear where they should. Always ^B any text that has been altered before printing it out.

With ^OE on, you have to type ^P- to enter a hard hyphen. Of course, you can also type ^OE-, if you're done entering soft hyphens.

Hiding Control Characters

The next command is ^**OD.** This is used to get a better picture of what a line will look like when printed out. There are many commands that can be embedded into text to alter how it prints out—to create boldfacing or underlining, for example. (All these commands are discussed in the next chapter.) These commands take up space on the screen.

For example, to boldface a word you put a ^B in front of and after it. So what appears on the page as **word** appears on the screen as ^Bword^B. WordStar will still accurately show you where each line will break, regardless of how many of these print control commands are in it. But lines that will end up the same length in a printout may have different lengths on the screen, so it is hard to visualize the finished text.

That's why WordStar gives you ^OD, which removes the print control commands from the screen. ^OD also hides soft hyphens that aren't at the end of a line. When ^OD is on, the screen says "print display now ON" which means that the display of print control characters is *on.* When ^OD is off, the screen says, "print display now OFF" which means that the print control characters are hidden (off). How's that for human engineering?

This is especially problematic if you try to edit with ^OD off (print control characters hidden). The results can be disastrous because you can easily delete print control characters without knowing it. Probably the easiest way to think of it is that ^OD should always be on (the way it comes) except for brief moments when you're checking formatting. As soon as you're done seeing how the text will look printed out (i.e., with ^OD off), go back to ^OD on. If you forget what the default for ^OD (or any other parameter) is, you can use the facsimile of the ^O menu at the beginning of this chapter to remind yourself.

Hiding Page-Break Display

The last formatting toggle is **^OP.** In normal operation, WordStar figures out where page breaks will fall and indicates them on the screen like this:

```
-----------------------------------------------------------------------P
```

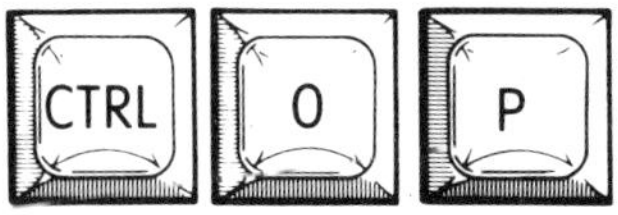

In the next chapter you'll also learn to put page breaks anywhere you want them; these are also indicated by the marker line above. ^OP turns off the display of page break lines and replaces the page number and line number on the status line with FC= and FL=.

FC stands for "file character count"; it gives you the number of characters from the start of the file to the cursor (+1, to be precise). Everything is counted—not just letters, numbers and punctuation marks, but carriage returns, spaces, print control characters, etc. **FL** stands for "file line count"; it gives you the number of lines from the start of the file to the cursor (again, +1).

So to find out the number of characters and lines in a file, first go to the end of the file (by typing ^QC). Then type ^OP. FC and FL will now show the values for the whole file. (You can also type ^OP and then ^QC; the order doesn't matter.)

10 Special Print Features and Dot Commands

WORDSTAR CAN underline text, strike it out, and print accent marks above it. It can stop in the middle of printing out and wait for you to tell it to go on (so you can change a type wheel or a ribbon.) It can switch from the black half of a ribbon to the red half and back again, or from 12 characters to the inch to 10 characters, without stopping. On printers that allow for it, Wordstar can produce **boldface** text, subscripts$_1$ and superscripts^2.

All these features and more are controlled by control characters or dot commands which are inserted into the text (embedded). These control characters are listed in the **^P** (for Print") menu:

```
^P    A:PRACTICE.DOC   PAGE 1   LINE 1   COL 01            INSERT ON

              <<<       P R I N T   M E N U        >>>

 ------ Special  Effects ------   |   -Printing Changes-    |  -Other  Menus-
 (begin and end) | (one time each) | A  Alternate pitch     |  (from Main only)
B Bold  D Double | H Overprint char | N  Standard pitch      | ^J Help   ^K Block
 S Underscore    | O Non-break space| C  Printing pause      | ^Q Quick  ^P Print
 X Strikeout     | F Phantom space  | Y  Other ribbon color  | ^O Onscreen
 V Subscript     | G Phantom rubout |   - -User  Patches- -  | Space Bar returns
 T Superscript   | RET Overprint line| Q(1)  W(2)  E(3)  R(4) | you to Main Menu.

L----!----!----!----!----!----!----!----!----!--------R
```

The ^P Menu

The first column of this menu lists the special effects that you order by putting a command at both the beginning and end of the text you want affected. **^PB** is the first of them.

Many new printers are capable of **microspacing** (also called **incremental spacing**). This means they can move in increments as small as 1/120th of an inch horizontally (and 1/48th of an inch vertically). If yours is one of them, WordStar provides you with boldfacing. It does this by going back to the start of the piece of text to be boldfaced, moving 1/120th of an inch to the right, and printing it again.

Boldfacing

CTRL P B

F6

A ^B is used to mark the beginning and the end of the text to be boldfaced. You insert the ^B markers by typing **^PB** or simply by hitting **F6.** Thus ^PBsyzygy^PB produces this on the screen:

    ^Bsyzygy^B

and this on paper:

syzygy

Doublestriking

CTRL P D

WordStar also lets you doublestrike. **Doublestriking** gives you a lighter kind of boldface. A ^D marks the beginning and end of the text to be doublestruck. You insert the ^D markers into the text by typing **^PD.** Thus ^PDparsec^PD produces this on the screen:

    ^Dparsec^D

and this on paper:

parsec (*slightly lighter than boldface*)

To produce doublestruck text, the printer is made to go back to the beginning of the marked piece of text and print it over again, but without moving over. On printers capable of microspacing, doublestriking can be used to contrast with, rather than substitute for, boldfacing (for example, for text that's intermediate in importance between boldfaced and normal text). On printers not capable of microspacing, ^PB and ^PD both produce doublestriking.

Doublestriking is sometimes used over an entire document. Doing this with a carbon ribbon produces an extremely sharp impression on the original, and lots of clear copies on multiple forms.

Underlining

CTRL P S

F5

WordStar lets you underline any amount of text, from one character on up, by using **^PS** (or **F5**) to insert ^S markers at the beginning and end. (Only non-blank characters are underlined; spaces and tabs are not.) So ^PSan albedo of .85^PS produces this on the screen:

    ^San albedo of .85^S

and this on paper:

an albedo of .85

Striking Out

^PX lets you strike out text with hyphens (-). So ^PXAldebaran ^PX shows on the screen as:

^XAldebaran ^X

and on paper as:

~~Aldebaran~~

Subscripts and Superscripts

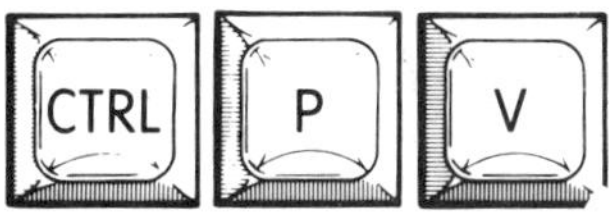

^PV produces subscripts. So H ^PV2 ^PVO shows on the screen as:

H ^V2 ^VO

and prints out as:

H_2O

You can vary how much below the line the subscript appears (with the dot command **.SR**). The default is 3/8ths of a (standard) line (i.e., 1/16th of an inch). On a printer that can't space less than whole lines, a subscript appears on the next line if it's blank, and on the same line as the rest of the text if it isn't.

^PT produces superscripts. So E = mc ^PT2 ^PT shows on the screen as:

E = mc ^T2 ^T

and prints out as:

$E = mc^2$

Since all these commands act as on/off toggles, be sure to always use them in pairs. Otherwise huge sections of your text will be unintentionally underlined, or boldfaced, or struck out.

The commands in the second column don't have this problem, because they're not toggles. Each of them works for one time only.

Overprinting Characters

For example, **^PH** is used to **overprint** a character, as you might want to do for a foreign word with a tilde or an umlaut or some

other kind of accent above it. So gre ^PHve produces:

gre ^H`ve

on the screen and

grève

on the page. It does this just once.

Overprinting is also useful for generating new and different characters, and for striking out a character with an X or a slash. So sto ^PH/j will produce:

sto ^H/j

on the screen and

støj

(the Danish word for "noise") on the page. Typing [^PH ^] will produce [^H] on the screen and a rectangular box on the page.

Non-Break Spaces

^**PO** serves a very useful function. If you think about it, there are two kinds of spaces that occur in text: regular spaces between words, which should be allowed to fall at the end of a line, and spaces that occur within, and are part of, the name of something or somebody.

These non-break spaces—as, for example, in names like Louis XIV—look funny when split between lines. All names like WW II should be kept all on one line. But it's a rare word processing program that has a way to do that. Fortunately, WordStar is one of them.

To insert a non-break space into a name or phrase, hit ^PO instead of the Spacebar where the space should be. On the screen the name will look like this:

PC ^ODOS

and on paper it will print out like this:

PC DOS

If there's no room for PC DOS to fit on one line, the whole name will be moved down to the next. The space between PC and DOS will never be at the end of a line.

Printing Special Characters

Formed-character printers (the ones that use daisy wheels or print thimbles) often give you the option of printing special characters, usually referred to as **phantom space** (20 hex) and **phantom rubout** (7F hex). The names and hexadecimal numbers need not concern you; what's important is that WordStar gives you access to two more print characters than you'd otherwise have.

The symbol that appears for phantom space and phantom rubout depends on the print wheel or thimble you're using. Usually phantom space prints out as a cent sign (¢) or a pound sign (£). You access it by typing **^PF.** ^F appears on the screen, and ¢ appears on the page. Thus, 27 ^F on the screen becomes 27¢ on paper. Phantom rubout usually prints out as a double underline or a graphic symbol such as ⏋. You access it by typing **^PG.** ^G appears on the screen and ⏋ appears on the page.

Overprinting Lines

WordStar also lets you overprint whole lines, for special effects. You can use this to cross out large sections of text with X's or slashes, as you sometimes need to do in legal documents. (But if you want to strike out a line with hyphens, it's easier to use ^PX.)

^P followed by ↵ calls up this feature. You type the ^P as the last character on the line you want overprinted, then hit ↵. Then you type the line you want to print over it, and end it with a regular return or allow it to wrap (unless you want a third line to overprint as well). The line to be overprinted will have a – flag at the end of it. So:

```
to her exclusive benefit in perpetuity^P(↵)
//////////////////////////////////////(↵)
```

shows on the screen as:

```
to her exclusive benefit in perpetuity        –
//////////////////////////////////////        <
```

and on the page as:

~~to her exclusive benefit in perpetuity~~

Changing Pitch

The commands in the third column of the ^P menu control changes that occur during printout. **^PA** ("Alternate Pitch") changes the number of characters to the inch for printers with microspacing.

So if you're doing a standard 10 characters to the inch (pica type), ^PA will change it to 12 characters to the inch (elite type), or to some other character pitch that you've specified with the .CW command (discussed later in this chapter).

^PN ("Normal Pitch") returns your printer to the standard pitch (or to some other pitch specified with .CW). ^PA inserts a ^A into the text at the point where the pitch will change, and ^PN inserts a ^N. Neither ^PA nor ^PN normally have any effect on printers without microspacing.

Changing Print Elements

If your printer is going to change the number of characters it prints to the inch, you're usually going to want the printout to pause so you can change the print element. **^PC** inserts a ^C into the text and WordStar stops the printout when it gets to that symbol. The words PRINT PAUSED appear on the screen. P (or, if you're editing a file, the ^KP command) re-starts the printout.

^C can be used in the middle of a line, or even several times in the same line if you want. Since some printers print bi-directionally, printout could stop at the wrong place if a line with a ^C in it was being printed from right to left. WordStar gets around this by always printing out lines that contain ^Cs from left to right.

Changing Ribbons

^C is also useful for changing the ribbon, so you can have various sections of the text print out in different colors. If you only need red and black, there's an even easier way to do it. Buy a two-color ribbon and use **^PY.** This acts as a toggle, switching printout from one color to the other. (Since you normally use black, the net effect is to switch you to red for a while.)

^PY inserts a ^Y into the text. So:

    I love the color ^PYR*E*D!! ^PY

will appear on the screen as:

    I love the color ^YR*E*D!! ^Y

and on the page as:

    I love the color R*E*D!!

with the word "R*E*D!!" in red.

Since you only get half as much mileage out of two-color ribbons, you should use them only if you're going to use the alternate color feature fairly extensively. ^PY works automatically on most formed-character printers, and can be activated on some non-formed-character printers by special procedures outlined in the WordStar installation manual.

Defining Your Own Print Features

Although WordStar has so many features it's sometimes hard to imagine that any other ones are possible, the program allows you to define four printer functions of your own. You define them when installing WordStar (or by modifying your installation), and call them up with **^PQ, ^PW, ^PE,** and **^PR.** Changing type fonts (on a printer like the Sanders Media 12/7 or Malibu Dual-Mode 200 where the same print head can produce different fonts) or activating a sheet feeder are two examples of what these commands can be used for.

Until they're installed, the user-defined printer functions do nothing. Sometimes standard WordStar installation of a printer will activate one or more of them. The WordStar installation manual tells you if this is the case, and gives you instructions for defining the functions yourself.

Dot Commands

That covers the commands listed on the **^P** menu, but only begins to explain all the ways WordStar lets you customize printouts. The rest of the controls are entered as **dot commands** (for a list of them, hit **^JD**). Dot commands are inserted into the text on lines that begin with a dot (i.e., a period). The dot tells WordStar that the line should not be printed literally, but rather treated as a command to be obeyed.

You can also use lines beginning with periods as **comments** on your text. You'll see them while editing, but they won't appear in the printout. If WordStar doesn't recognize something on a dot line as a command, it assumes it's a comment and ignores it.

This can cause a problem if a period in your text accidentally ends up at the beginning of a line. So if your printout is missing a single line, check the disk file to see if that line has a period in the first column.

The WordStar convention is to start comment lines with two dots, but any line starting with a dot not followed by a command will work.

All dot command parameters—margin widths, line spacing, the number of characters to the inch, etc.—are set at standard default values. Thus, you can print out an entire document without entering any dot commands at all—if your tastes in printouts are identical to MicroPro's.

If they're not, you can re-set many of these default values with the installation program. (See the installation manual to find out how.)

Dot commands will be shown in caps in this book, to make them easier to pick out of the text. But, as with all WordStar commands, they have the same effect when typed lowercase (which is easier).

Each dot command must be entered on a separate line that has a period in the first column. If a number is part of the command, you can type it right next to the command (.CP5), or separate it by one space (.CP 5) or many spaces (.CP   5). Any additional text on the same line is assumed to be a comment and will not be printed out (unless it's a header or footer, which I'll discuss later).

If you make a mistake typing a dot command, WordStar will put a ? in the last column of the line. If that doesn't get you to fix it, the line will be treated as a comment and ignored during printout.

Without further ado, let's go on to the dot commands themselves.

Line Height

.LH (for "Line Height") controls line spacing on printers with microspacing. Line spacing is measured in 48ths of an inch, because that's the smallest vertical motion a printer with microspacing can make. The default is 8 (8/48ths of an inch), which equals 1/6th of an inch, or 6 lines to the inch. LH allows you more precise line spacing than the single-, double-, and triplespacing you get with ^OS.

Page Length

.PL ("Page Length") tells WordStar the length of the sheets of paper you're using (or, with fan-fold paper, the distance between the perforations). PL is measured in lines, so it depends on LH. The default is 66 (which, since the default for LH is 6 lines to the inch, equals 11 inches).

Top Margin

.MT ("Margin, Top") sets the number of lines from the top of the page to the first line of text (the main text, not the header—I'll cover this in a bit.) The default is 3 lines, which sounds like too little. This is because WordStar counts from where the print head is positioned when you put the first sheet of paper in, not from the top of the sheet. So two people can use the same top margin but get different-looking printouts, depending on how they position the paper in their printers.

With this and all the other margin parameters, you should experiment until you get a printout that looks the way you want it to.

Bottom Margin

.MB ("Margin, Bottom") sets the number of lines from the last line of (the main) text to the bottom of the page. The default is 8 lines, some of which actually fall on the next page, unless you position your print head right at the perforation between sheets. With single sheets you can't even do this, because the paper won't go under the bail (the thin bar with the rubber rollers on it). WordStar allows about 3 extra lines so you can get your paper under the bail.

Headers and Footers

.HE ("header") is used to generate headers automatically (lines of text at the top of each page). The text begins one space after the dot command; that is, ".HE " is skipped over, then the text begins. So, for example:

```
.HE Mastering WordStar
```

will put the header "Mastering WordStar" in the upper left corner of each page. To put it in the upper right corner, you'd type:

```
                                        .HE  Mastering WordStar
```

adjusting the placement by inserting spaces. Remember that since ".HE " doesn't print, your header appears on the dot command line four spaces to the right of where it will appear on the page.

To center the header, you'd type:

```
.HE              Mastering WordStar
```

(again, centering it by inserting spaces).

It's also possible to have a left and a right header:

```
.HE Mastering WordStar          Arthur Naiman
```

Once set up, a header continues to be printed at the top of each page until turned off. (You do that by typing .HE with nothing after it.) You can change the header as often as you want. The default for .HE is for there to be no header.

.FO ("footer") works the same way for footers (lines of text at the bottom of each page) as .HE does for headers. The only difference is the default. If you don't specify a footer, WordStar will print the page number in the center of the footer line. If a footer is specified, the page number isn't printed. You can also turn off this automatic page number with the **.OP** ("omit page") command.

You can control the distance of the header line from the top of the page (and, therefore, from the first line of text) with the **.HM** (for "header margin") command. This positions the header *within* the top margin. So if MT is set for 6 and HM is set for 2, you'll get two blank lines, the header, and three more blank lines, and then the text. (The default is 2 lines.)

The footer margin is set in the same way, with **.FM**. Again, this positions the footer *within* the bottom margin. So if MB is set for 6 and FM for 2, you'll get the last line of text, two blank lines, the footer, and three more blank lines before the bottom of the page—or, more accurately, before the line on which the print head started on the first page you printed out. (The default is 2.)

Page Numbering

Page numbering normally starts at 1 and goes up, but you can reset it with the **.PN** ("page number") command. Just follow the command with the number you want to start with. If page numbering has been turned off with the .OP command, .PN will turn it back on again. If you want to turn page numbering back on but don't want to change the page number, type .PN with nothing after it. Numbering will pick up where it left off.

.PC ("page column") followed by a column number will move the page number from the center of the footer line to the column specified. Thus .PC 5 would place the page number five spaces in from the left margin.

If you want the page number at the top of the page, insert the **#** symbol into your header where you want the page number to appear. (You'll also need to use .OP to turn off the default page numbering in the footer line, unless you've specified some other footer.) # prints the current page number, whatever that is, on each page. You can also print the page number as part of a footer line you specify, by inserting the # symbol—for example:

.FO Working draft three, revised specs, page #

{in the printout, # becomes a number}

.PN can be used to change page numbers that are produced by #. It works just the same way as it does for the default page numbering that's centered in the footer line.

As if all this weren't enough, WordStar gives you a way to alternate page numbers so they appear on the right side of odd numbered pages and the left side of even numbered pages (and thus are always toward the outside edge of the page). You do this with **^K.** This character in a header or footer suppresses printing of blank spaces whenever the page number is even. So if you have a dot command line which reads:

.HE ^K   Page #

WordStar will kill those spaces whenever the page number is even, thereby putting the number on the left:

Page 2

and will leave them in whenever the page number is odd, thereby putting the page number on the right:

Page 3

Headers and footers can contain boldfacing, underlining, etc. The \ symbol lets you print characters that normally do not appear. For example, suppose you wanted the # symbol to appear in a footer. If you just typed it in, you'd get the page number, instead of the symbol. A \ before the #, however, would tell WordStar not to interpret it as a command but just to print it as is. Thus:

.FO Page \# #

would print out as:

Page # 26 {or whatever}
in the bottom left corner of each page.

Page Offset

.PO ("page offset") controls how many columns your text is moved over from the left side of the printer. This offset is in addition to the left margin set by ^OL and any other spaces or indentation in your file. This is so you don't start printing too close to the left edge of your paper. PO is measured in columns (the default is 8). The actual width of these columns, and therefore of the total page offset, depends on what the character spacing is set at.

Character Width

.CW ("character width") controls how many 120ths of an inch is allotted to each character (120ths of an inch because that's the smallest horizontal distance printers with microspacing can move). You can set CW for both the standard and alternate pitch; .CW will change whichever happens to be in effect (as selected by ^PA and ^PN) when the .CW command is given. (.CW has no effect on printers without microspacing.)

The default for standard pitch is 12 (12/120ths of an inch, or 10 characters to the inch—i.e., pica type). The default for the alternate pitch is 10 (10/120ths of an inch, or 12 characters to the inch—i.e., elite type).

Or you can set each of them for whatever you want. One use for .CW is setting characters farther apart than normal, for emphasis, as you might want to do in a title. Pica type at a setting of 15 has this effect. (Don't forget to adjust the right margin for the new character spacing, or you may print right off the right side of the page.)

The .HE, .FO, .PC, and .PO commands all depend on the character spacing in effect at the point where you give the command. Thus, the following sequence of commands will produce headers with a character width of 15 and text with a character width of 12, starting one inch (10 columns at 10 characters to the inch) from the left edge of the paper:

```
.CW 15
.HE The Way It Spozed to Be                    James Herndon
.CW 12
.PO 10
  At least it looks like a school . . . old, dark, the same brown
window shades all pulled exactly three-quarters of the way
down . . .
```

On the page, it will look like this:

The Way It Spozed to Be James Herndon
At least it looks like a school . . . old, dark, the same brown window shades all pulled exactly three-quarters of the way down . . .

The chart on the next page shows the various print parameters and their relations to each other.

Microjustification

WordStar normally justifies to the right margin by putting tiny spaces between letters and words. This is called **microjustification.** Microjustification improves the appearance of text and you normally want it turned on (which is the default). But if you're printing out a table, microjustification might throw off the alignment (if, for example, soft spaces somehow got into the table lines during word wrap or reforming).

.UJ OFF will turn microjustification off, so that the printed text is spaced exactly as it is on the screen. **.UJ ON** turns it back on again. In any case, lines that weren't formed with word wrap, or reformed with ^B when ^OJ was ON, are never microjustified. With .UJ off, word wrapped or reformed text appears with spacing inserted only between words, not within them.

Forcing a Page Break

WordStar automatically goes to a new page when it has filled all the lines of text between the top and bottom margins. But sometimes you want to move to a new page before the old page is full. One example is when you're starting a new chapter of a book, or section of some other kind of document.

To force a page break, you use **.PA** (for "page"). Simply type in .PA on a line by itself wherever you want the page to break. Follow the command with a carriage return and WordStar will immediately draw a line on the screen to show you where the page ends.

Preventing a Page Break

Sometimes you want a table or some other piece of text (like a subtitle and the first line—at least—of the paragraph following it) to stay together on one page. If there's room for it on the present page, you want it printed out there. If there isn't room for it on the present page, you want the whole thing moved to the next page and printed out there.

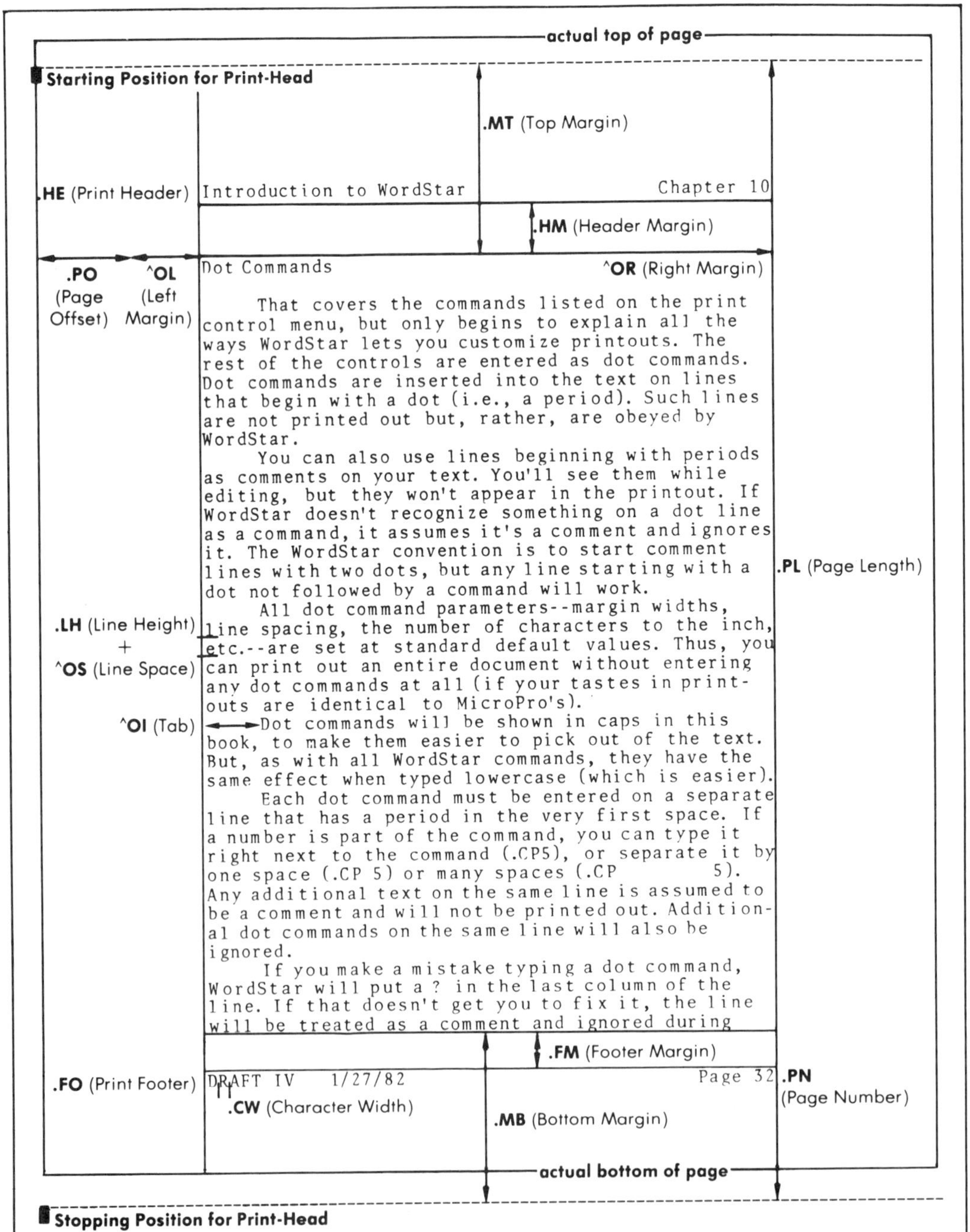

Printing Parameters

Obviously .PA isn't going to do this for you. That's the domain of **.CP** (for "conditional page"). You put the .CP command right before the piece of text you want kept on the same page, and you indicate on the command line the number of lines that must stay together (counting skipped lines, double or triple spacing, etc.).

When WordStar runs across .CP, it pauses and it counts the number of lines remaining on the page. If that's less than the number following the .CP, WordStar generates a .PA and goes on to the next page. If the number of lines left on the page is more than (or equal to) the number following .CP, it just continues printing on the same page.

Let's say you want to keep the following poem (including its title and author) together on one page:

An Immorality

Sing we for love and idleness,
Naught else is worth the having.

Though I have been in many a land,
There is naught else in living.

And I would rather have my sweet,
Though rose-leaves die of grieving,

Than do high deeds in Hungary
To pass all men's believing.

—Ezra Pound

All you have to do is put a line that reads .CP 15 right in front of it, and it will be kept together.

Another good use for .CP commands is to keep the first line of a paragraph from printing out alone at the bottom of a page. To do that, you put .CP 2 (or 3, if you want) in front of every paragraph in the file.

A generous use of .CP commands helps keep a document looking good regardless how much text you put in or take out of it, and regardless of how often you reform it.

Before you enter a dot command, it's a good idea to check its default value (so you'll know where you're starting from when you pick a new value). As I mentioned earlier, ^JD will give you an onscreen list of WordStar dot commands, what they do, and their default values (or see page 170).

11 Printing Out

WORDSTAR LETS YOU EDIT one file while printing out another, unless your system has only 64K. Even with more memory, the response speed is slowed down, so it's probably a good idea to edit while printing only when the editing is minimal, such as reviewing a file or making minor changes in it. If you hear your disk drive working, or see the message:

DISK WAIT

on the status line. When this happens, stop typing until WordStar catches up with you. If you want faster responses, you can temporarily stop the printout, as described below. (You can also execute most opening commands while printing out.)

Instead of menus, the print function uses questions to get the information it needs. You call up these questions with the **P** command from the opening menu, or the **^KP** command from the editor. (M is used to print out under the optional MailMerge program, which is covered in the next chapter.)

Naming the File to be Printed

The first question WordStar asks you, quite logically, is:

NAME OF FILE TO PRINT?

(Although WordStar's print function is designed primarily to handle its own files, it can also be used to print out files prepared by other programs, as long as they're in the "ASCII" character code. There are a few minor differences in how such files get formatted, and they may have to be edited and formatted through WordStar before successful printing.)

After you type the filename, you have two choices: you can hit ↵, and be asked a series of questions about the printout. Or you can hit Esc, and skip the questions; printout will begin immediately with the default answers to the questions in effect. The default values produce a hard copy printout of the whole file, with normal formatting and form feeding, and without pauses at the end of each page. (All these parameters are explained in a bit.)

If you choose Esc, make sure your printer is turned on, with continuous-form paper correctly positioned in it, because printout will start immediately. (It will probably take you a few tries to get the paper right, so that the text will be printed where you want it on the page.) If this is your first time printing out, don't use Esc. You'll want the printout to stop after the first page, so you can adjust the paper if necessary.

```
P            not editing

 ^S=delete character   ^Y=delete entry   ^F=File directory
 ^D=restore character  ^R=Restore entry  ^U=cancel command

   NAME OF FILE TO PRINT? TEST.DOC

   For default press RETURN for each question:
      DISK FILE OUTPUT (Y/N):
      START AT PAGE NUMBER (RETURN for beginning)?
      STOP AFTER PAGE NUMBER (RETURN for end)?
      USE FORM FEEDS (Y/N):
      SUPPRESS PAGE FORMATTING (Y/N):
      PAUSE FOR PAPER CHANGE BETWEEN PAGES (Y/N):
   Ready printer, press RETURN:

DIRECTORY of disk A:
  PRINT.TST         WS.COM    WSMSGS.OVR    WSOVLY1.OVR
```

The P Command Display

Printing to Disk

If you hit ↵ after the filename, WordStar will ask you the following questions:

DISK FILE OUTPUT (Y/N):

If you want the printout to end up as a new file on disk, rather than as a hard copy on paper, answer Y (or y, or ^Y) to this question. WordStar will then ask:

OUTPUT FILE NAME?

Type the name you want for this new file, and WordStar will put it on the disk, leaving the printer completely alone.

The new file will be a "printed version" of the original; that is, all the dot commands will be executed, rather than displayed. For example, a line like:

```
.HE The Yankee and Cowboy War
```

will disappear; instead, the header itself will appear at the top of each page. You can review this "printed" version on the screen (it's easier to see what's going on than with on-screen formatting), and if you want, send it directly to the printer later on.

If you type any key other than Y, WordStar will send the printout to the printer.

Where to Start

```
START AT PAGE NUMBER (RETURN for beginning)?
```

You can specify some page other than 1 for the printout to begin at. You'll definitely want to do this if the printout was interrupted for some reason—some difficulty with the printer or paper, for example, or if you want to go back to correct a mistake you didn't catch until you saw it on paper. After you enter the page number, press ↵. There will be a delay while WordStar works its way through the file to the page you've specified. (If you're starting on a page far into a long file, this delay can be quite long.)

If you want to start at the beginning, hit ↵. A zero or a one, followed by a ↵, has the same effect.

Where to Stop

```
STOP AFTER PAGE NUMBER (RETURN for end)?
```

WordStar also lets you specify some page other than the last for the printout to stop after. To tell WordStar to print the entire file, just hit ↵.

Paging with Form Feeds

```
USE FORM FEEDS (Y/N?)
```

Normally, WordStar goes from one page to the next by telling the printer how many lines to space (you've already told it what you want the top and bottom margins to be). But some dot-matrix printers work faster if they find the top of the page (or "top-of-form," as it's called) themselves. To let them do that, answer Y to this question. (But be sure you understand how your printer works and set the appropriate switches to notify the printer of where the top of the first page is and what the length of each page is.)

This will make WordStar ignore the line spaces; instead, it will tell the printer to find the top of the next page itself, and move there. If your printer uses form feeds, you don't have to set the paper length (the .PL command).

Suppressing Formatting

SUPPRESS PAGE FORMATTING (Y/N)?

If you want to proofread the dot commands in your file, rather than see their effects, answer Y to this question. This suppresses all page formatting—top and bottom margins, headers, footers, page numbers, etc. The printout will run right across the folds in the paper between the pages. To suppress page formatting, answer Y to this question. The dot commands in your file will appear on the paper just as they do on your screen. (However, most print control characters—^B for boldfacing, ^H for overprinting, etc.—have their normal effects.) In addition to editing dot commands, this option can be used to print out files that are already formatted, either because they were produced by a program other than WordStar, or because they've been "printed to disk" with the DISK FILE OUTPUT option above.

Pausing between Pages

PAUSE FOR PAPER CHANGE BETWEEN PAGES (Y/N):

This option lets you print out on single sheets of paper, rather than continuous forms. If you answer Y for yes, print out will stop after each page, and the words PRINT PAUSED will appear on the status line. To make the print out start again (after you've changed the paper), hit P or ^KP again. If you answer this question with anything but a Y (y, ^Y), WordStar will print out continuously, without stopping between pages.

Having answered all these questions, you're ready to actually begin printing. Make sure your printer is turned on, and set "on-line" if that's required. (Some printers with keyboards let you use them as typewriters if they're set "off-line" or "local.") Make sure the paper is in the printer and positioned vertically so that each page will begin printing where you want it to.

Then all you have to do is hit any key at all. Your file will start printing out, and the screen will return the opening menu or the main menu, whichever one you were at when you began printing.

Interrupting the Printout

If you want to stop the printout, type either P or ^KP. The following message will appear on the screen:

TYPE "Y" TO ABANDON PRINT, "N" TO RESUME, ^U TO HOLD:

If you want to stop the printout completely at this point, hit Y. If you want to go on again (for example, after adjusting the paper), hit N. If you want to go back to the opening or main menu to do other things, and then start printing out again right where you left off, hit ^U. This pauses the printout until you hit P or ^KP again. You can issue as many commands as you want before going back to printing out.

After you press P to stop the printout, there will probably be a delay while the printer empties its buffer. Don't make the mistake of pressing P again in an effort to get the printer to respond, because WordStar will think you want it to start printing again. Sometimes printout pauses on its own. There are several reasons why this happens:

1. When you edited the file, you inserted a ^C character into the text, so that you could change a daisy wheel or print thimble.
2. You answered "yes" to the PAUSE FOR PAPER CHANGE BETWEEN PAGES? question above, and you're now between pages.
3. You're "printing to disk" (i.e., you answered "yes" to the DISK FILE OUTPUT? question above) and you've just gotten a DISK FULL error message.

When printout is paused, the words PRINT PAUSED appear in the status line. If you're working off the main menu, the words TYPE ^KP TO CONTINUE PRINT will also appear. And that's exactly what you do when you want to start printing out again (if you're working off the opening menu, you type P). Naturally, before you give the command to resume, you should change the daisy wheel, or put in a new sheet of paper, or clear more space on the disk—whichever is called for.

Printout may also pause because the printer is nearly out of paper or ribbon. (In this case, the words PRINT PAUSED probably won't appear on the screen.) Exactly what happens in this situation varies with the particular printer. Some stop completely. Some print right off the end of the paper. Others just sound an alarm or show a warning light.

Even if you respond in time and add paper before the last page, you can lose some words or get uneven spacing between lines. If this happens, the only way to get a clean copy is to stop the current print (with P or ^KP), then restart it, answering the question START PAGE? with the number of the first page you want reprinted.

12 *Merging Files with MailMerge™*

THE MAILMERGE PROGRAM, available at additional cost from MicroPro, works with WordStar to produce **repetitive documents.** It's designed to save you a lot of work in any application where large portions of the text are the same from one document to the next, but where some information in each document varies.

Some examples of this sort of document are **customized form letters,** where the name, address, and possibly other information vary while the rest of the letter stays the same; reports or proposals that go to different agencies, where pieces of boilerplate—standard text used in a variety of situations—are interspersed with different introductory and connective material and arranged in different order; and mailing labels, where everything changes except the format.

MailMerge also makes it possible for you to chain several files during printout, with continuous page numbering and no required page breaks between them, and to print out both letters and envelopes from the same mailing list with a single command. MailMerge substitutes for WordStar's normal print function, and can do all the same things (except for printing a file while editing another).

If you want to send letters to just part of your mailing list—say, just to the people who live in Peoria—you can instruct MailMerge to select those addresses and skip all the others in the list. You can even tell it to include a particular paragraph in some letters, but leave it out of others.

Two different sorts of information are always present any time you use MailMerge—the **matrix** (or matrix document or invoking document) and the **variables.** The matrix document is what stays the same from one printout to the next. Within it are markers that tell MailMerge where to insert variables, which represent information that changes from one printout to the next. MailMerge recognizes these markers because they're surrounded by ampersands (&s).

Writing a Form Letter

So—let's say you are writing a form letter that you want to customize for various recipients. It might look something like this:

May 12, 1985

&Mr – Ms& &FirstName& &LastName&
&CompanyName&
&Address&
&City&, &State& &Zip&

Dear &Mr – Ms& &LastName&,

Should you have the good fortune to become one of my creditors, you will have gained membership in a very select club . . .

Variable Names

The words and phrases between the &s (*Mr – Ms, FirstName, LastName,* etc.) are called **variable names**. You have a lot of latitude in choosing a variable name, but there are some rules:

1. It must be no more than 40 characters long. (In practice, you'll want to save yourself typing by keeping variable names short. Some of the ones shown above are long only for the sake of clarity).
2. It must begin with a letter (capital or lowercase).
3. The rest of the name must be composed of capital and/or lowercase letters, and/or numbers. You can also use hyphens if you want. Nothing else is allowed. In particular, spaces and any punctuation other than hyphens, aren't allowed.

So instead of calling the second variable *FirstName,* you could call it: *Firstname, firstname, FIRSTNAME, first-name, Name-1,* or *name-one.* But you couldn't call it *1st-name* (variable names must start with a letter), *Name 1* (no spaces allowed), or *first*name* (no symbols allowed except for hyphens).

Variable Values

What gets substituted for the variable name when the letter is printed out is called the variable's value. For example, "Smith" might be a value for the variable name *LastName.* For the variable *CompanyName,* the value might be "Corporate Androids, Inc." For the variable *Address,* the value might be "1100 Enterprise Drive". And so on.

(Don't be confused by the word "value." In common language, it's used to refer to a number, but in computerese, it means any group of characters, any string. That's because to a computer, any group of characters, even a name like Vincent Van Gogh, is just a bunch of numbers.)

Variable values can be up to 200 characters long, and they can contain any sort of character at all. Thus they can be as short as a single letter, or as long as a paragraph. (In fact, a whole file can be substituted for a variable; this will be discussed later.)

When MailMerge substitutes a variable value for a variable name, it also removes both of the ampersands (&s) that surround it. By the way, you can use ampersands as part of your regular text too. When MailMerge runs across an ampersand, it looks for another one nearby (within 40 spaces, the maximum length of a variable name). If it doesn't find one, it just prints the ampersand and goes on. If it does find a second ampersand, but doesn't recognize what's between them as a variable name, it prints both ampersands and goes on.

There are three major ways MailMerge finds out what value to substitute for a variable name: by looking on a data list for it, by inserting another file from the disk, or by asking you. Since looking on a data list is the most common procedure for form letters, we'll cover that one first.

Data Files

For the purposes of MailMerge, a **data file** is a list of **records** containing variable values. Each record is made up of one set of variable values and ends with a carriage return. (In other words, carriage returns separate the records.) Within each record, the values are separated by commas; these are called **separator commas.** Spaces may be inserted after the commas to improve readability. However, they are usually omitted, because in long data files, spaces make for slower processing and inefficient use of disk space.

If a value has a regular comma within it, you put quotes around the value so that MailMerge will know that it isn't a separator comma. The quotes drop off when the value is printed out. You should also use quotes if you want to include a space at the beginning or end of a value. Otherwise, such spaces will be ignored. (In fact, you can use quotes around each value if you want, but why make work for yourself?)

A record in a data file might look like this:

```
Mr.,John,Smith,"Corporate Androids, Inc.",1100 Enterprise
Drive,City of Industry,CA,91744
```

(The record doesn't have to appear as one line on the screen, just so long as there aren't any carriage returns in it.)

If you use the letter cited above as the matrix, MailMerge will combine the data file with it to produce a customized form letter that looks like this:

May 12, 1985

Mr. John Smith
Corporate Androids, Inc.
1100 Enterprise Drive
City of Industry, CA 91744

Dear Mr. Smith,

Should you have the good fortune to become one of my creditors, you will have gained membership in a very select club . . .

If you use MailMerge to combine a data file containing 100 records with a matrix document, you'll get 100 versions of the matrix, each (like the example above) containing the variable values from a different record in the data file. The number of records in the data file determines how many letters will be printed out (although you can request two or more letters for each record).

Each record is divided into **fields**, which are the areas between the separator commas where the variable values go. The record above has 8 fields. The first field contains the value for *Mr – Ms;* the second contains the value for *FirstName;* and so on. Values have to be in exactly the same order (that is, in exactly the same fields) in each record, so MailMerge knows where to find each one.

You can use WordStar to create and edit data files, but if you plan to be doing a lot of this sort of work, it might make sense to buy a data entry program. Such programs make entering and checking the data easier. But for now (and for data files of moderate length), WordStar is perfectly adequate.

Matrix Documents

Now—exactly how do you go about creating a matrix that will generate form letters or other repetitive documents?

.DF

Obviously, one thing you have to do is tell MailMerge which data file you want to pull your variable values from. You do this with the dot command **.DF** (for "data file"), followed by the name of the data file. So, for example, the dot command:

```
.df mainmail.lst
```

tells MailMerge to get whatever variable values are asked for in your matrix by looking at the data file called MAINMAIL.LST (which, judging from its name, is probably your main mailing list).

MailMerge looks for the data file on the currently logged drive. But you can also have it look on another drive, by putting that drive letter in front of the filename. If the currently logged drive is A, the command:

```
.df b:mainmail.lst
```

will tell WordStar to look for the data file MAINMAIL.LST on drive B, instead of the logged drive A.

MailMerge also lets you change disks so you can insert a new one that has the data file on it. You do that by putting the word CHANGE after the name of the data file. So:

```
.df b:mainmail.lst change
```

will make MailMerge pause before starting to print out the merged letters and show this message on the screen:

```
Insert diskette with file B:MAINMAIL.LST then press RETURN:
```

At that point, you put the disk with the data file on it into drive B and hit ↵.

.RV The other things you have to tell MailMerge in order to get it to merge a matrix with a data file are the names of the variables you're going to be using, and what order they appear in the data file's records. This information is given by means of another dot command, **.RV** (for "read values").

The .RV command is followed by the names of the variables, in the order in which they occur in each record in the data file. The names are separated by commas and optional spaces.

So the .RV dot command line for the example above would look like this:

```
.rv Mr–Ms, FirstName, LastName, CompanyName,
Address, .rv City, State, Zip
```

If all the variable names won't fit on one .RV line, either because the names are too long or because there are too many of them, you can use two or more .RV lines. MailMerge will just go on to the second line after it has exhausted the variables in the first. If the .RV line calls for more variables than there are in each data file record, MailMerge will move to the next record to get them. If the records have more variables than the .RV line calls for, MailMerge will ignore the extras. (Normally, you don't want either of these things to happen.)

As was mentioned above, the variables in the .RV command line must be in the same order as the variables in the data file records. In the matrix document itself, however, the variables can be in any order, and each can be repeated as often as you want.

You can also have variables listed in the data file, and therefore in the .RV line, that don't appear in a particular matrix. That way you can use the same data file for a number of different matrix documents, pulling out just the variables that are needed for a particular document. Or you can list variables that never appear in a matrix—for example, the numbers of each record in the data file. So:

```
.rv RecordNumber, Mr–Ms, FirstName, LastName
.rv CompanyName, Address, City, State, Zip
```

will work fine with:

```
1,Mr.,John,Smith,"Corporate Androids, Inc.",1100 +
Enterprise Drive,City of Industry,CA,,91744
```

in a matrix file where the variable *RecordNumber* never appears.

Remember that if a particular variable is in the data file record, it *must* be listed on the .RV line whether or not it's called for in the matrix you're working with. Otherwise, all the variables will be one field off, and you'll get things like "Dear Mr. 6105 North Winthrop".

The .DF and .RV lines are embedded at the beginning of the matrix, before any repetitive text or variables. The .DF must always come first.

Page Numbering

There are some other dot commands you'll probably want at the beginning of the file too. For example, if you're typing a one-page letter, you don't want the page number 1 to appear at the bottom. Use .OP to suppress it.

If you have more than one page and do want them numbered use .PN 1 on the first page, so each letter will begin its numbering at 1 again. (If you don't use .PN 1, all the letters will be numbered consecutively.) You should always use either a .OP command or a .PN command at the beginning of a form letter matrix (or, for that matter, the matrix for any repetitive document).

Page Breaks

The .PA command tells WordStar to end the page. You should always put this at the end of any matrix, so the next document will begin at the top of a page. (Chain printing, discussed later on, is an exception to this rule.)

Comments

You may also want a comment at the start of a matrix file, to remind you what the matrix is for (beyond the maximum eleven letters of the file name). Comment lines start with two periods; whatever follows is ignored by WordStar—neither printed out nor obeyed. A comment line might look like this:

```
..form letter to creditors
```

Printing Out Merged Documents

Once you've made all these preparations, printing out a series of merged documents is easy. Basically, all you have to do is give MailMerge the name of the matrix file.

You call up MailMerge by hitting **M** under the opening menu. The **M command display** appears:

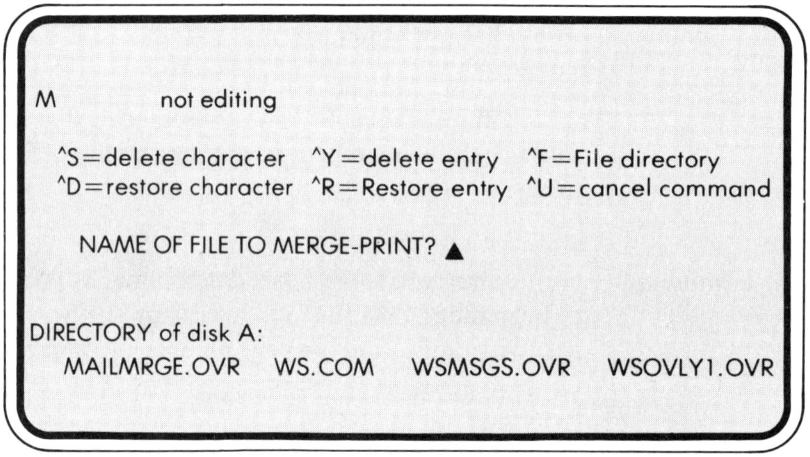

The M Command Display

You enter the name of the matrix file and hit ↵. A series of questions—similar to those asked for normal WordStar printouts and covered in the last chapter—follows. There's an extra question in the list:

NUMBER OF COPIES (RETURN for 1)?

Remember that this means "number of duplicate copies of each merged document." If you have a data file of 20 records, and if you answer 3 to this question, you'll get 60 documents—3 for *each* record.

Here, as with regular printing, you can avoid all the questions by pressing Esc, instead of ↵, after typing in the filename. MailMerge will then give you the defaults. But if you're doing form letters on individual sheets of letterhead, remember to answer Y to the PAUSE BETWEEN PAGES question.

While MailMerge is printing, it puts this message on the screen:

P = STOP PRINT

P is the only command that can be given during merge-printing.

If there are any error messages during the printout, they'll appear on the bottom half of the screen. If you've told MailMerge to ask you for information during the printout (how to do that is discussed below), these requests will also appear on the bottom half of the screen. If there's room, the file directory will remain displayed (assuming you haven't turned it off at the opening menu).

```
  M          not editing

^S=delete character     ^Y=delete entry     ^F=File directory
^D=restore character    ^R=Restore entry    ^U=cancel command

 NAME OF FILE TO MERGE-PRINT? TEST.DOC

 For default press RETURN for each question:
     DISK FILE OUTPUT (Y/N):
     START AT PAGE NUMBER (RETURN for beginning)?
     STOP AFTER PAGE NUMBER (RETURN for end)?
     NUMBER OF COPIES (RETURN FOR 1)?
     SUPPRESS PAGE FORMATTING (Y/N):
     PAUSE FOR PAPER CHANGE BETWEEN PAGES (Y/N):
 Ready printer, press RETURN:

DIRECTORY of disk A:
   MAILMRGE.OVR    WS.COM    WSMSGS.OVR    WSOVLY1.OVR
```

Merge-Print Questions

When the printout pauses—either because you hit P, or because there's a ^C in the file, or because you're between pages and have to put in a new sheet of paper, the opening menu comes back on the screen. To resume printout, hit P again.

Samples Here's a sample matrix file, the data file (composed of three records) it links with, and the output they produce together under MailMerge:

SAMPLE MATRIX FILE{Filename: CREDLTR.MMG}

```
..form letter to potential creditors/MailMerge matrix file
.op
.df mainmail.lst
.rv RecordNumber, Mr–Ms, FirstName, LastName
.rv CompanyName, Address, City, State, Zip

                                              May 12, 1985

&Mr–Ms& &FirstName& &LastName&
&CompanyName&
&Address&
&City&, &State& &Zip&

Dear &Mr–Ms& &LastName&,

   Should you have the good fortune to become one of my
creditors, you will have gained membership in a very select
club . . .
```

SAMPLE DATA FILE {Filename: MAINMAIL.LST}

```
1,Mr.,John,Smith,"Corporate Androids, Inc.",1100 Enter-
prise Drive,City of Industry,CA,91744

2,Ms.,Ananda,Moondaughter,"Fuzzy, Furry & Soft",14
Grotto Lane,Aumsville,Oregon,97325

3,Prince,Relth,Gryzaxq,Sirian Mission to the Planet Ear-
th,"Algonquin Hotel, 59 West 44th Street",New
York,NY,10036
```

SAMPLE OUTPUT {produced by CREDLTR.MMG and MAINMAIL.LST}

May 12, 1985

Mr. John Smith
Corporate Androids, Inc.
1100 Enterprise Drive
City of Industry, CA 91744

Dear Mr. Smith,

Should you have the good fortune to become one of my creditors, you will have gained membership in a very select club . . .

* * * * *

May 12, 1985

Ms. Ananda Moondaughter
Furry, Fuzzy & Soft
14 Grotto Lane
Aumsville, Oregon 97325

Dear Ms. Moondaughter,

Should you have the good fortune to become one of my creditors, you will have gained membership in a very select club . . .

* * * * *

May 12, 1985

Prince Relth Gryzaxq
Sirian Mission to the Planet Earth
Algonquin Hotel, 59 West 44th Street
New York, NY 10036

Dear Prince Gryzaxq,

Should you have the good fortune to become one of my creditors, you will have gained membership in a very select club . . .

Asking for Values

Sometimes you don't want your variable information drawn from a data file (if, for example, you have no reason to keep a record of the names and addresses you're sending letters to, or if you want to insert information that isn't in a data file). MailMerge gives you a second option that covers such situations—you supply the variable values yourself, right during printout.

.AV

The dot command that lets you do that is **.AV** ("ask for value"). .AV works like .RV, except that there is only one variable name in each .AV line, and you can specify whatever word (or words) you want to be prompted with when MailMerge asks you to supply the variable value. As with .RV, the variable names in a .AV line must match the variable names embedded in the matrix document.

For example—let's say you're an elementary school teacher writing letters home to the parents of each of the kids in your class. There's a phrase in each letter (i.e., in the matrix document) that reads:

```
I am &modifier& pleased to report that your little &brat-
name& has made a great deal of progress in &subject&.
```

At the start of the matrix file, you have three dot commands:

```
.av modifier
.av bratname
.av subject
```

(As with all variable names, these must start with a letter and contain only letters, numbers and hyphens—no spaces or other symbols.)

The .AV tells MailMerge to ask you for the values rather than to look for them in a data file. When MailMerge comes to ".av modifier", it will ask:

MODIFIER?

You respond by typing in "very" and hitting ↵. As you're asked for each value in turn, your previous responses (if any) remain on the screen, for example:

MODIFIER? very
BRATNAME? Craig
SUBJECT? geography

When MailMerge has finished asking all the questions you've set up at the start of the file, it will print out a letter, substituting the answers you supplied for the variables in the matrix text (for example, "I am very pleased to report that your little Craig has made a great deal of progress in geography.").

As with any variable values, these can be several words (or even sentences) long. For example:

MODIFIER? thrilled, delighted and—believe me, Mrs. Kulick—more than merely
BRATNAME? Rosalyn

SUBJECT? learning to control her tendency to make sarcastic remarks

would produce:

> I am thrilled, delighted and—believe me, Mrs. Kulick—more than merely pleased to report that your little Rosalyn has made a great deal of progress in learning to control her tendency to make sarcastic remarks.

Multiple Copies with .AV

With .DF and .RV commands, MailMerge keeps printing out letters until it has gone through the entire data list. With .AV commands, however, the default for the number of letters to print is one. After the .AV questions have been answered and the letter printed out, MailMerge returns you to the opening menu. So if you want to generate several letters from the same matrix, you have to do one of the following things:

1. Type M from the opening menu and run through the series of print questions for each letter you want to print. (The next two techniques save you this hassle.)
2. The first time you run through the questions, answer NUMBER OF COPIES with 347 (or any other large number). When you've done all the letters you want, hit P to stop printing out.
3. Put the following dot command on the last line of your file:

   .FI filename

   (where "filename" is the name of the file you're working with. So if this file were called ENDTERM.RPT, the last line would read ".FI endterm.rpt"). This will make MailMerge go back to the beginning of the file every time it reaches the end of it. (.FI commands have many other uses, which I'll get to in a little while.)

There's one problem with these endless printout loops (techniques 2 and 3 above): stopping them. If you type P when you're being asked a .AV question, MailMerge will think it's the answer to the question and not a command. So:

MODIFIER: p

won't stop the printout; it will produce:

I am p pleased to report that . . .

To get around that difficulty, hit ↵ and then P as close to each other as possible. ↵ will terminate the .AV question, and the P will sneak through before MailMerge can ask another one. (This technique is also useful when you change your mind and decide, in the middle of a series of .AV questions, not to go ahead with printing the file.)

When you're typing out several letters, and the response to an .AV question in the letter you're on is the same as it was in the last letter, ^**R** will retype that last response for you, saving you from having to type it over and over again.

If you want to clear the screen of the .AV questions and answers for the last letter, so the ones for the present letter will start at the top of the screen, embed the command **.CS** (for "Clear Screen") at the top of your matrix letter.

Prompting Yourself

Sometimes the variable name, followed by a question mark, isn't what you want to prompt yourself with in answering an .AV question. You can substitute other text by putting it between .AV and the variable name. The prompting text must be enclosed in single or double quotes and followed by a comma. When the .AV question is asked, just the text in quotes will appear; the variable name and the question mark are omitted. Thus:

```
.AV "Type the two-letter code for the state:", STATE
```

will produce the following prompt (instead of "STATE?"):

```
Type the two-letter code for the state:
```

Checking Yourself

You can also limit the number of characters MailMerge will accept as a valid response to a .AV question. You might want to do that to force yourself to use two-letter state codes, for example, or to make sure you didn't slip while entering a zip code and type too many numbers. You do this by putting a comma after the variable name and adding a number which stands for the maximum number of characters you want MailMerge to accept.

So the command line:

```
.AV "Type the two-letter code for the state:", STATE, 2
```

will not only tell you to type the two-letter code, it will keep repeating that instruction if you type more than two. (The maximum length option, and the special prompt option, can be used independently of each other. You don't need one to have the other.)

Merging Whole Files

In addition to .RV and .AV, there's another main way that MailMerge works—by inserting a whole other file into the matrix you're using. You do this with the **.FI** ("file insert") dot command, followed by the name of the file you want inserted:

```
.FI DISCLAIMER.TXT
```

.FI is great for boilerplate—pieces of text that are used in several different documents. Let's say you have three paragraphs you often use, word for word, in the contracts you prepare. One says that what's written in the contract constitutes the whole agreement; another says that if one part of the contract is found to be illegal, the rest of it will still stand; the third details the procedure to be followed if either party thinks the contract has been breached. You make each of these paragraphs into a separate file—call them WHOLEAGR-.PAR, SEVERABL.PAR, and BREACH.PAR—and insert them wherever you need them with .FI commands:

```
. . . insofar as the same are assignable.
.fi severabl.par
.fi breach.par

This contract shall be binding upon, and shall be for the ben-
efit of, the licensee and also the licensee's heirs, executors,
administrators and assigns, and likewise upon and for the
benefit of the licensor and also their successors and assigns.
.fi wholeagr.par
```

There's even a way to insert boilerplate files into the middle of paragraphs, but that's too advanced for an introductory book like this.

Creating Command Files

.FI also lets you create **command files**—that is, files composed entirely (or mostly) of dot commands. One use for command files is to save yourself retyping print parameters for various documents. You just create a file for each different format that includes all the print parameters for that format (BUS-LTR.PRM, PERS-LTR.PRM, LABELS.PRM, etc.). Then when you're printing out a personal letter, say, you just insert the file that contains the print parameters for a personal letter.

```
..wedding thank you notes
.fi pers-ltr.prm
  &date&

Dear &name&,
etc.
```

Chain Printing

What is probably the most useful command file enables you to print multiple files, with consecutive page numbering and without requiring page breaks between them. This is something that WordStar, without MailMerge, can't do.

Let's say you're printing out a long report. You make each section a separate file: SECTION1, SECTION2, etc. Then you create a command file—call it MULTPRNT. MULTPRNT looks like this:

```
.fi section1
.fi section2
.fi section3
etc.
```

There's nothing in the file but .FI commands. When you call up MailMerge—with M from the opening menu—you give MULTPRINT as the name of the file you want to print out. MailMerge inserts SECTION1, followed by SECTION2, etc. (These files shouldn't have .PN 1 commands in them. And they don't need to end with .PA unless you want a page break between them.)

You can put a drive letter in front of a filename (b:section3) to let MailMerge know where to find the file, and if the report is really long, you can also ask MailMerge to pause while you change disks:

```
.fi section1
.fi b:section2
.fi b:section3 change
.fi b:section4
.fi b:section5 change
```

Mailing Labels

A file to print mailing labels is a command file of a sort—it contains nothing but dot command and variables:

```
. .format for one-across labels
.mt 0
.mb 0
.df customer.lst
.rv name, companyname, address, city, state, zip
(RETURN)
&name&
```

```
&companyname&
&address&
&city&, &state& &zip&
(RETURN)
```

(The .mt 0 and .mb 0 kill the top and bottom margins; the line spaces in the file are all you want there.)

You can create a Matrix file similar to the one used above for mailing labels and use it to format data files—so you can read them more easily than when all the fields are squeezed together without any spaces between them.

Alternating Letters with Envelopes

MailMerge also allows you to print out letters and envelopes alternately. Here's an example of a command file that does that:

```
..letter and envelope program/birth announcement
.op
..insert stationery here
^C
.pl 42
.mt 8
.df xmascard.lst
.rv FirstName, FirstAndLastName, Address, City, State, Zip

                                                  August 8, 1985


Dear &FirstName&,


   On August 4th, at 8:25 p.m., we were blessed with a
beautiful baby girl, 8 lbs, 4 oz . . .
.pa
 .pl 24
.mt 12
..insert envelope here
 ^C
&FirstAndLastName&
&Address&
&City&, &State& &Zip&
.pa
```

The page length (.PL) for the note paper is 42 lines (7 inches, since this is single-spaced—6 lines to the inch—by default). The "page" length for the envelope is 24 lines (4 inches). ^C stops the printout twice in each cycle, once to insert the note paper and once to insert the envelope. .PA forces page breaks, so that the text will be positioned correctly on both the note paper and the envelope (by the .MT—top margin—commands).

Conditional Printing

Sometimes you'll want to include a piece of "conditional" text in some letters, but leave it out of others. If you have MailMerge version 3.3, you can do this by inserting two dot commands in the matrix document.

The command that comes before the conditional text always begins with either .IF (for "if . . .") or .EX (for "except when . . . ") followed by one or more conditions to be met for the text to be included or left out. The end of the conditional text is marked by an .EF dot command.

For example, the **conditional command**

```
.IF &state& = "California" GOTO
```

tells MailMerge to omit the text which follows when it prints letters to people with addresses in California. When MailMerge comes to this command and the variable value in the STATE field is California, it skips to a second dot command, **.EF**, and resumes printing.

Starting a conditional command with the dot command .EX has the opposite effect. So the conditional command

```
.EX &state& = "California" GOTO
```

translates "Skip this section of text except when the state is California." This would cause Mailmerge to *include* the conditional text in all letters to addresses in California.

You can specify a value for any variable name listed after .RV or .AV in the matrix document. So you can include or omit paragraphs in letters to specified cities, streets or zip codes, as well as to people with particular first or last names. The variable value is always enclosed in quotation marks, and the variable name is enclosed in σ (ampersand symbols). There must be a space between each item in the command, except that you don't have to put a space before and after the = sign.

There's no limit to the number of conditional commands you can put in a matrix document—as long as each .EX or .IF has a corresponding .EF command. (Make sure you don't put them in with nothing between them.)

Conditional printing can also be used to tell MailMerge to print out letters to some people but not to others. You simply place an .IF or .EX command at the beginning of the matrix letter (after the .DF and .RV commands, but before the body of the letter), and put an .EF command at the very end (after the .PA command). MailMerge treats the entire letter as a piece of text to be included or omitted.

Complex Conditional Commands

You can also specify more than one condition at the same time.

```
.IF &city& = "San Francisco" .OR. &city& = "Los Angeles" GOTO
```

means "If the city is San Francisco or Los Angeles, skip this section of text and start printing again at the .EF command."

Similarly,

```
.EX &city& = "San Francisco" .AND. &street& = "Mission" GOTO
```

would result in the text being included only in letters to Mission Street addresses in San Francisco. (You have to put a period both before and after the AND or OR that connects the two conditions.) Using this method, you can string together several conditions (as long as the command fits one line and doesn't exceed 100 characters).

Comparison Characters

Sometimes you might want to specify many different values for a variable, rather than just a few. A common example is when you want to send letters to a part of the country covered by a broad range of zip codes. It would get tedious to type each zip code into a conditional command.

To get around this, MailMerge lets you specify a *range* of values for any variable. If you wanted to send letters to all zip codes between 49521 and 98367, for example, you would insert the conditional command

```
.EX &zip& > "49521" .AND. &zip& < "98367" GOTO
```

at the beginning of the matrix letter. The symbols > (for "greater than") and < (for "less than") are called **comparison characters.** Altogether there are eight different comparison characters that you can use to define the value of a variable. (See the chart below.)

Character	**Meaning**
=	equal
<>	not equal
<	less than
>	greater than
<=	less than or equal to
>=	greater than or equal to
=>	equal to or greater than

You can also specify ranges of letters (in alphabetical order). So if, for example, you want to send report cards to students whose last names begin with C through G, you could insert the command

```
.EX &bratname& >= "C" .AND. &bratname& <= "G" GOTO
```

at the beginning of the matrix letter.

Labels

Sometimes you'll have more than one conditional command in at the same point in a matrix document. (For example, you might want letters going to Connecticut to skip the following three paragraphs.) Since each .EX or .IF command must have a corresponding .EF command, you'll need to let MailMerge know which .EF to skip to before it continues printing. You do this by adding a **label** after .EF, and the same label after GOTO in the conditional command. A label can be anywhere from one to twenty characters long—just as long as it never starts with a number and never includes spaces (although there must be one space between it and the rest of the command). For example, in the conditional command

```
.EX &zip& = "22307" GOTO NEXTSECTION
```

"NEXTSECTION" is the label that also appears in the corresponding end command

```
.EF NEXTSECTION
```

Labels are also needed when pieces of conditional text overlap—that is, when a second .IF or .EX comes before the first .EF. Even when there's no overlap, it avoids possible confusion if you add labels whenever you have multiple conditional commands in a matrix document.

That may seem rather complicated to you, but it's just a shadow of what MailMerge can do. There's a lot more to say about MailMerge, but this chapter is already the longest in the book. Hopefully it has given you a good sense of some of MailMerge's capabilities.

13 Checking Spelling with SpellStar™

SPELLSTAR IS AN OPTIONAL MicroPro program that works within WordStar to **proof** files—that is, it checks the spelling of all the words in the file. It does this by taking each word and trying to match it with the words in a **dictionary.** If the word isn't listed in the dictionary (or dictionaries) SpellStar is using, SpellStar assumes the word is misspelled.

Since SpellStar's dictionary can't include all the words you might use, the list of words it thinks are misspelled is bound to include names of people and places, technical terms and obscure words, as well as words that are genuinely misspelled. As you'll see in a while, SpellStar gives you different ways to handle each.

To get you started, SpellStar comes with a dictionary of about 20,000 words, called **SPELSTAR.DCT.** You can:

- *add* words to SPELSTAR.DCT;
- *delete* words from it; and
- *create* whole new dictionaries of your own.

Naturally, SPELSTAR.DCT and any other dictionaries you may create will take up a lot of room. In the discussion that follows, I'll be talking as if your computer uses 8" disks. If it uses 5¼" disks, you'll need to work with three disks instead of two (swapping them in and out of the drives), because mini-disks have less capacity. Refer to the SpellStar Reference Manual for details about using 5¼" disks.

Before you learn how to create and modify dictionaries, let's see how SpellStar proofs a file using SPELSTAR.DCT.

Calling up SpellStar

You get to SpellStar through WordStar. For the purposes of this discussion, both the WordStar and SpellStar programs should be on drive A, and a blank disk should be in drive B. From the opening menu, hit **S.** The following message will appear on your screen:

NAME OF FILE TO CHECK / ADD TO DICTIONARY?

You can enter the name of any file you want to proof, but it probably makes sense to start off with the sample file that comes with SpellStar. This is called SAMPLE.TXT and is with the rest of the programs on disk A, so answer the question by typing:

a:sample.txt

Now the screen will show the main SpellStar menu, called the **operations menu.**

```
O P E R A T I O N S

C  – Check spelling
M  – Maintain dictionary
X  – Exit to WordStar no-file menu

Operation? ▲
```

The Operations Menu

This menu gives you three choices; it lets you:

- check the spelling of a file (**C**);
- create a new dictionary, or modify an old one (**M**); or
- forget about SpellStar entirely and go back to WordStar (**X**).

Since you want to check the spelling of a file, hit C. The screen will change to show the **spelling check menu.**

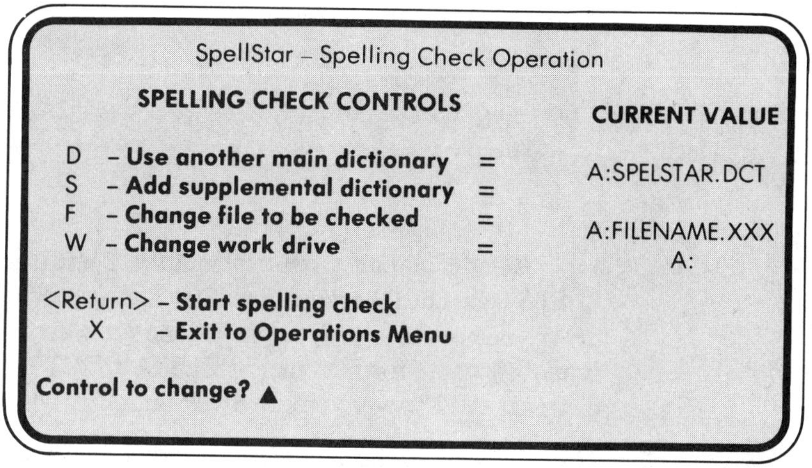

The Spelling Check Menu

On the right, under the words CURRENT VALUE, are listed, from top to bottom:

1. the name of the dictionary you'll be checking the words against;
2. the name of the file you'll be proofing; and
3. the drive you're logged onto.

You can specify a different dictionary, text file or drive if you want to at this point. If you don't, SpellStar will use the ones listed here.

Choosing a Dictionary

D is the first of a series of commands on the left of the menu. It lets you pick another dictionary to check the words against. Type D to see how you go about doing that. The following message appears on the screen:

```
D—Dictionary: A:SPELSTAR.DCT This is the current dictionary.
                             Enter the drive, filename,
                             and/or extent of the main
                             dictionary to use.
```

This is all pretty self-explanatory. There's an "A:" in front of SPELSTAR.DCT because SpellStar can use dictionaries on either drive; you need to specify where the one you want is located. "Extent" is another name for file type. SPELSTAR.DCT is SpellStar's default dictionary. Whenever you run SpellStar, that's what's listed.

To change the dictionary you want SpellStar to use, just type in the new name. You can also change the drive or the file type, all independently of each other. SpellStar is so smart that it will recognize which part of the name you mean to change, without your having to tell it. So if you type:

b: (followed by ↵, of course)

SpellStar will change the name of the dictionary to B:SPELSTAR.DCT.

If you type:

.dic(↵)

SpellStar will change the name of the dictionary to A:SPELSTAR.DIC (or B:SPELSTAR.DIC if you have already changed the drive).

If you type:

devil's(↵)

SpellStar will change the name of the dictionary to A:DEVIL'S.DCT (or B:DEVIL'S.DIC if you made the above changes). (The clue, as you've already figured out, is the presence of a colon (:) or a period (.). Still, it's a nice touch, even if it isn't really artificial intelligence.)

You can also type the whole replacement name at once, for example:

```
b:devil's.dic(↵)
```

But, at this time, you don't actually want to substitute a different dictionary, since you don't have one to substitute. So type in "a:spelstar.dct" (if you made any changes) and hit ↵.

Using a Supplemental Dictionary

The next command on the left, **S,** lets you add a supplemental dictionary. SpellStar doesn't limit you to just one dictionary when proofing. It will look for the words in your text file in two separate lists if you want—the main dictionary and the supplemental dictionary.

Why not just combine two lists into one big dictionary? Because the supplemental dictionary can be composed of specialized terms, which vary depending on the nature of the text file, while the main dictionary is composed of general terms, which are common to all text files. For example:

MAIN DICTIONARY

the	two
and	threw
why	please
not	help
time	I'm
river	a
we	prisoner
both	in
recognize	spelling
necessity	checker
to	dictionary
too	

SUPPLEMENTAL DICTIONARIES

Legal	*Crime*
pursuant	Cosa Nostra
tort	consigliere
retainer	cut
Medical	*Military*
episiotomy	neutralize
tonsilectomy	scenario
fee	appropriation
Business	*Writing*
C.O.D.	deadline
F.O.B.	overdue
percentage	advance

(These wouldn't be in random order in the actual dictionaries, of course.)

If you're writing a business letter, you use the main dictionary plus the special supplemental dictionary of business terms; if you're writing a contract, you use the main dictionary plus the special supplemental dictionary of legal terms; if you're writing your editor, you use the main dictionary plus the special supplemental dictionary of terms that explain why you don't have the material done on time.

Another use for supplemental dictionaries is to list proper names—people in your company, place names in the area you're writing about, etc. SpellStar can then catch misspellings of them too.

When you hit S, the screen looks like this:

```
S — Supplement:     This is the current supplemental
                    dictionary. Enter the drive,
                    filename, and/or extent of the
                    supplement to use.
```

There is no filename shown, because the default is to use the main dictionary only. If you wanted to use a supplemental dictionary too, you'd just type the name in. Entering or changing any part of a name works just the way it does under D (above). Since we're not going to use a supplemental dictionary to proof SAMPLE.TXT, we want to leave the supplemental dictionary name the way it is—blank. You do that by simply hitting ↵.

Proofing a File

F lets you change the name of the file you're proofing, if you've changed your mind in the ten seconds since you entered that name in response to SpellStar's question: FILE TO CHECK / ADD TO DICTIONARY?

Another use is when you want to proof several different files in a row (it saves you from having to start over). F works the same way as S and D. Since we want to proof SAMPLE.TXT, just hit ↵ to leave things as they are.

When SpellStar proofs a file, it creates temporary files that are just as large as the file you're proofing. The drive it does this on is called the work drive. You have to decide which disk has room for the work files (SpellStar assumes the logged disk unless you tell it otherwise).

If the disk in the logged drive doesn't have enough room for the work files, send them to the other disk, using **W**. Here's a use for that blank disk in drive B if the disk in drive A is too full to handle the work files. You can check how much room is left on both disks with PC DOS's CHKDSK command (you get to it by going back to the opening menu and giving the R command).

You might as well change the work drive, since the disk in drive B, being blank, is bound to have more room on it than the disk in drive A. Hit W and type B (no need for a colon or ↵ here).

X (as always) will drop what you're doing and move you back a level—in this case, from the spelling check menu to the operations menu. (You can do this without affecting any of the changes you've made, as long as you don't exit WordStar itself.) But you want to run the spelling check now, so hit ↵ in response to the question "Control to change?".

The screen will now look like this:

```
Spellstar—Spelling Check Operations
[Checking A:SAMPLE.TXT]

SpellStar is now checking your document for misspelled
words.

Number of words in document. . . . . . . . :    422
Number of different words. . . . . . . . . . :    261
Number of words in main dictionary. . . : 21182
Number of words in supplement. . . . . . :
Number of dictionary words checked. . : 21182
Number of misspelled words. . . . . . . . . :     28
Total number of misspellings. . . . . . . . . :
```

Before it does any proofing, SpellStar counts the number of words in the text file and puts them on the first line above. Then it tells you how many *different* words make up that total. (So, to pick an absurd example, if you were proofing a file composed of the word "obsession" repeated a thousand times, the first line above would register "1000" and the second line would show "1".)

Line 3 tells you the number of words in the main dictionary, and Line 4 tells you the number of words in the supplemental dictionary, if one was specified.

As SpellStar proofs the file, the number in Line 5 (number of words checked) changes. (If you get bored sitting and watching the screen, go do something else until the check is done.)

When SpellStar has finished, the number in Line 6 will indicate how many different words in the file SpellStar couldn't find in the dictionary(ies). This will include not only typos and misspelled words, but also proper names and obscure words that are not in the dictionary(ies). (These should be called "unmatched" rather than "misspelled" words.)

The last line is used to indicate how many occurrences of the "misspelled" words counted in Line 6 appear in the text (so if you've misspelled "separate" as "seperate" three times in the file, it will count for 1 on Line 6, and 3 on Line 7).

The screen will now look like this:

```
SpellStar has completed proofreading your document.
Enter "L" to list the misspelled words.
Enter <Return> to flag errors in your text.
Enter "R" to abandon the check and restart.
```

Marking and Correcting Misspelled Words

The words have been found but not flagged (marked) in the text. Hitting ↵ will tell SpellStar to flag them for you. If you want to see a list of them first, hit **L** and they'll appear on the screen. If the file you proofed was SAMPLE.TXT, the list will look like this:

```
AA CH WS SAN ATTN DISCO TOM'S TYPOS WIT'S WRKNG
BILOXI CALVIN DISCOS RAFAEL SURVAY KEYTOPS MAUREEN
HOTSTUFF JUMPSUIT ONSCREEN PROGRAMM HICCUPING
WHISKEY'S WORDSTAR'S FREEWHEELING CORESPONDENCE
INTERNATOINAL INSUBODRINATION
Enter <Return> to flag errors, "R" to restart.
```

When you hit ↵, SpellStar removes the list from the screen (if you called it up), fills in the total number of occurrences on the last line, and puts the following message at the bottom of the screen:

> SpellStar has flagged the misspellings in the text.
>
> Enter <Return> to correct errors in the text, "R" to restart.

Now you can go through the file and correct the errors. Hit ↵ again. If you used SAMPLE.TXT, the screen will look like this:

```
    A:SAMPLE.TXT     PAGE 1  LINE 3  COL 42  ACTION       (F/B/I/D/S)?▲
    F - Fix word       D - Add to dictionary
    B - Bypass word    S - Add to supplemental dictionary
    I - Ignore word

L- - - -!- - - -!- - - -!- - - -!- - - -!- - - -!- - - -!- - - -!- - - -!- - - -!- - - - -R

                                    April 1, 1985

                                          Calvin P.      ▲Hotstuff
                                          ^@Freewheeling Enterprises
                                          ^@Biloxi, Mississippi

MicroPro ^@Internatoinal
1299 Fourth Street
^@San ^@Rafael, California 94901
      ^@Attn: Customer Service

Dear Sirs:

        I want to start by telling you that I think WordStar is a
```

Words Flagged by SpellStar

The cursor will be at the first error, and additional errors in the text will be flagged with the ^@ symbol in front of them. When you move the cursor to any of the other flagged words, the ^@ disappears and the word is either reversed (black on white) or dimmed—depending on your terminal. You just go through the file and make whatever corrections are necessary.

You have two basic choices when you get to a word—you can change it, or leave it the way it is. To change it, hit **F**. Recognize that menu? You are now in the WordStar editor and you can use any WordStar command to make whatever changes are necessary. When you're done, **^L** will put you back in SpellStar and move the cursor to the next word.

If you want to leave a word unchanged, it's because the word is, in fact, correct. SpellStar just doesn't happen to have it in the dictionary (or supplemental dictionary) you used. Some of these words are obscure and unlikely to come up in any other context, so it's silly to clog up your dictionaries with them. When you get to such a word, hit **I.** The word will be ignored, and SpellStar will skip over any future occurrences of it that have been flagged.

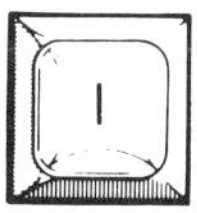

Other words are likely to come up elsewhere, and would be useful additions to a dictionary. If you want such a word to be added to a main dictionary, hit **D.** If you want it to be added to a supplemental dictionary, hit **S.** (The dictionaries can be the ones you used to proof this file, or any other ones you want.) With both D and S, you'll be asked to verify that you do indeed want to add the word to the dictionary, and haven't just hit the wrong key accidentally. If the word in question is "uvula," SpellStar will ask:

```
Add to Dictionary: UVULA (Y/N)?
```

Answer Y and the word will be added.

(As you can see, if you're running SpellStar while reading this, SpellStar automatically moves you to the next flagged word as soon as it finishes executing the command you gave it. You don't need an additional command, except in the case of F.)

Sometimes you're not sure if you want to add a word to a dictionary or just ignore it. Or you may not be sure whether to change a word, because you haven't decided how you want to spell it (Roumania, Rumania or Romania, for example). In any case, you don't want to be bothered making the decision now. That's what **B** is for. It lets you bypass a word temporarily and come back to it later.

When you've gone through the whole file, hit **^QL.** You'll see

this on your screen:

```
To search for misspelled words, enter one of the following—
RETURN=search forward, B=search backward, G=from
start of file:
```

These commands take you back through the file, stopping at words you bypassed (with the B command) the first time around. You don't want ↵, because that will take you forward through the file from where you are now, which is at the end—in other words, you won't go anywhere. **B** and **G** will both get you through the whole file, G will move you forward from the start, B will move you backward from the end.

(Don't be confused by the two B commands. The first tells SpellStar you want to bypass a word and is used when you're moving through the file from one marked word to the next. The second comes after you've finished correcting the file and hit ^QL to go back to the words you bypassed.)

At each of the bypassed words, you can now decide to fix (F), ignore (I), or add to a dictionary (D or S), just as you did above. When you're finished correcting the proofed file, save it with ^KD. This takes you back to the WordStar opening menu.

In the directory below the menu, SAMPLE.TXT (or whatever the name of the file you proofed) has the spelling corrections in it. SAMPLE.BAK is a copy of the file before you ran it through SpellStar. SAMPLE.ADD is composed of all the words you didn't fix—you either ordered SpellStar to ignore them, or to add them to a dictionary. Now I'll cover how you take those words out of SAMPLE.ADD and put them into your dictionaries.

Creating and Revising Dictionaries

SAMPLE.ADD is a **word file**—that is, a list or collection of words you want to add to your dictionaries (or make into a separate dictionary). In order to add words to a SpellStar dictionary, or to create a new dictionary, you must always start with a word file. It can be an .ADD file created by SpellStar. You can type one out yourself. You can buy a disk with a dictionary on it. Or you can just take a whole text file and have SpellStar add every word in it to a dictionary (SpellStar will discard the duplicates).

Wherever your word file comes from, you start adding it to SpellStar at WordStar's opening menu. Hit S to get to SpellStar. You're asked:

NAME OF FILE TO CHECK / ADD TO DICTIONARY?

Before, when you were proofing a file, you answered with the name of the file you wanted to check. Now, when you're adding a word file to a dictionary, you respond with the name of the word file (let's assume it's SAMPLE.ADD). SpellStar will assume the word file is on the logged disk, unless you tell it otherwise (e.g., b:sample.add).

Now the SpellStar operations menu appears.

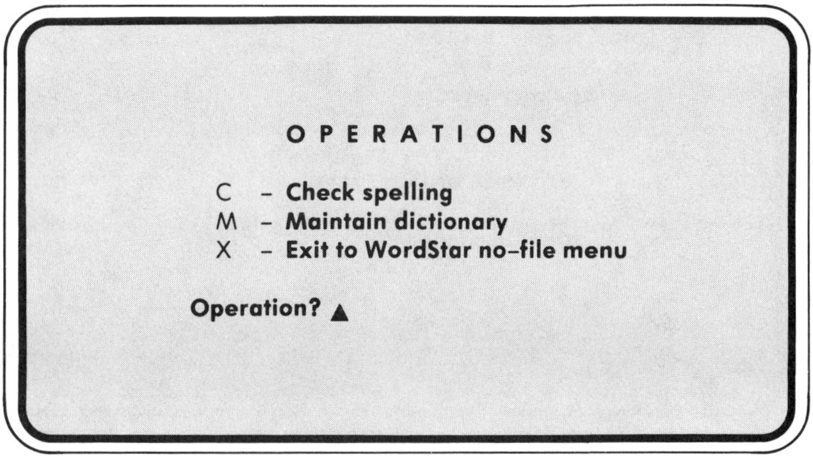

The Operations Menu

Last time you chose C, in order to check a file. This time select answer **M,** because you want to maintain your dictionary(ies). This brings on the **dictionary maintenance menu.**

As with the spelling check menu, the "current values" are listed on the right. First is the name of the word file you're adding, followed by the dictionary you want to add it to. Next is the name you want to give the new, updated dictionary (i.e., the old dictionary + the new additions). Last is the drive you want to use for the temporary sort files. I'll cover them one at a time.

```
        SpellStar - Dictionary Maintenance

        DICTIONARY MAINTENANCE CONTROLS                     CURRENT VALUE
F  - Change word file to use                       =    A:FILENAME.XXX
D  - Change dictionary to update                   =    A:SPELSTAR.DCT
U  - Change name of new or updated dictionary      =    A:
W  - Change work drive for sort                    =         A:

        DICTIONARY MAINTENANCE OPTIONS
N  - Create a new dictionary                       =         NO
A  - Add words                                     =         NO
T  - Delete words                                  =         NO
C  - Combine add/delete                            =         YES
S  - Use "S" words from ".ADD" file                =         NO
L  - List dictionary words                         =         NO

<Return>  - Start dictionary maintenance.
   X      - Exit to Operations menu

Control or option to change? ▲
```

The Dictionary Maintenance Menu

Since you just finished entering the word file's name, it's unlikely you'll want to change it. But if you do, **F** will allow you to, in exactly the same way as you changed current values on the spelling check menu. (You can change each part—drive, file name, type—independently. Refer back to the section if you don't remember how to do it.)

Just as SPELSTAR.DCT is the default dictionary to check files with, so it is the default dictionary to update. SPELSTAR.DCT appears on both the spelling check menu and the dictionary maintenance menus whenever you first bring them up. If you want to add the

word file (or part of the word file) to another dictionary, you can change this value with **D.** If you want to create a completely new dictionary, just leave this value blank.

If you leave the value for "new or updated dictionary" blank (as it is by default), SpellStar will overwrite the old dictionary with the new, revised dictionary, giving it the same name and putting it on the same drive. Other possibilities, using the **U** command, are:

- to change the name (to MAIN/REV1.DCT, say);
- to change the drive to which the new file goes (so that a file with the same name will appear on each drive, one being the new one and the other the old one; or
- to change both the name and the drive of the new file—so you have, say, A:SPELSTAR.DCT (the old file) and B:MAIN/REV1.DCT (the new file).

In combining a word file with a dictionary, SpellStar requires a temporary sort space approximately the size of the word file. If there isn't enough room for that on A, sort on a different drive. Use the **W** command to change it.

Farther down the screen are the **dictionary maintenance options.** SpellStar assumes you going to add *and* delete words to an already existing file; if you want to do something other than that, these option commands will let you. First you're asked if you're creating a new dictionary; if that's what you want to do, hit **N.** The screen will read:

N — New option: NO	Create a new dictionary using words in word file. Enter <Y>es or <N>o.

If you answer Y, the value will turn to YES and, simultaneously, the value for "combine add/delete" will go to NO and "add words" will go to YES (since you obviously can't delete words from a new dictionary).

If you want to update an existing dictionary by only adding words and not deleting any—and that's what I'll assume in the rest of this discussion—hit **A.** The screen will read:

```
A – Add words NO    Add all words in word file to
                    dictionary. Enter <Y>es or <N>o.
```

Respond with a Y. "Add words" will go to YES (and "combine add/delete" to NO).

You can also decide to only delete words (using **T**). You do that with a word file made up of the words you want to delete. It's a good idea (although not necessary) to label this file with the type .DEL, so you don't forget and add these words by mistake. Then you toggle **T** from no to yes, and proceed just as you would if adding (which is described below).

If you've changed from the default of adding and deleting, but now want to go back to it, use **C.** How, you may wonder, can SpellStar both add words to and delete words from a dictionary at the same time? How will it know which to add and which to delete? It's simple: if a word in the word file already exists in the dictionary, SpellStar deletes it. And if it isn't already in the dictionary, SpellStar adds it. As a safety precaution, SpellStar will put each word to be deleted on the screen and ask you to OK it. For example:

```
[SCROD]
This word is in the dictionary. Should it be deleted? (Y/N)?
```

But it only does this check if you're both adding and deleting words. If you're just deleting, it doesn't ask for your OK.

Adding and deleting at once, rather than separately, saves time. But this time through, we're just going to add words.

If your word file is an .ADD file created by SpellStar, SpellStar will add to the main dictionary only the words you marked D. However there might be words in there you marked S, because you wanted them to go into a supplemental dictionary. If the dictionary being updated is a supplemental dictionary, use the **S** command to add the S words instead of the D words.

If you want SpellStar to show you what words it's adding from the word file to the dictionary while it's adding them, use **L.** The screen will now look like this:

```
SpellStar is now creating or updating your dictionary:

      Number of words in word file..................: 3
      Number of different words in word file..........: 3
      Number of words in dictionary being updated....:
      Number of words added to dictionary..........:
      Number of words deleted from dictionary.......:
      Number of words in new or updated dictionary...:

                                  [List of update words]
POLYANDROUS MULCT NEOTONY


Enter <Return> to proceed, "R" to restart
```

Obviously lines 1 and 2 will only be different if you're using a text file for your word file. If you're using a dictionary you purchased, a list of words you typed up, or an .ADD file created by SpellStar, the duplicates will have already been eliminated.

Below the six "number" lines are listed the words to be added. After you've looked at the words to be added, hit ←┘. Then SpellStar will begin listing—one screenful at a time—all the words in the new, revised dictionary. As SpellStar updates (i.e., revises) the dictionary, the appropriate numbers will appear on the last six number lines, (which are all more or less self-explanatory).

Neither the list of update words nor the new dictionary listing is in alphabetical order. Instead, words are grouped by length—all the one-letter words first, then all the two-letter words, etc. Within each group, the listing is alphabetical. So if you were looking for the word "wrong," you'd wait for the five-letter words and then look under *W.* "Wrongs" would be with the six-letter words, "wronged" with the seven-letter words, "wrongful" with the eight-letter words, etc.

When combining the word file and the dictionary, SpellStar stops after each screenful, and continues only after you call up a new screenful. But this can be changed, as the message that appears under the list indicates:

"space" = continue, "C" = continuous listing,
"^L" = stop/start list

So—if you want to go on to the next screenful of words, hit the **SPACEBAR.** If you want the list to scroll continuously, hit **C.** If you want the list to disappear completely and for SpellStar to revise the dictionary at top speed, hit **^L.**

When the revision is finished, the following message will appear:

SpellStar has completed the dictionary maintenance.
Enter <Return> to return to WordStar. "R" to restart.

Using **R** will allow you to go back to the dictionary maintenance menu and add other words from this word file to another dictionary—for example, the S words to a supplemental dictionary. All you'd have to do in that case is change the name of the dictionary to update (or create a new one), hit S, answer Y, and hit ↵.

When you've added (and/or deleted) all the words in a word file from the appropriate dictionaries, you should kill the word file so it doesn't clutter up your disk. You should also delete the old version of the dictionary you revised, once you're sure the new version is the way you want it.

There is one reason to save an .ADD file. In addition to the words you marked D and S, it includes the words you marked I. While these words won't be added to any dictionary, they will be ignored when you recheck that text file again (as you might want to do after you added to it or changed it). It saves time to have them ignored. But once you're sure you're not going to proof a text file again, dump the .ADD file that corresponds to it.

To get back to the WordStar opening menu when you're done with SpellStar, hit ↵.

Appendix A Summary of WordStar Commands

Moving the Cursor

The Keys Used

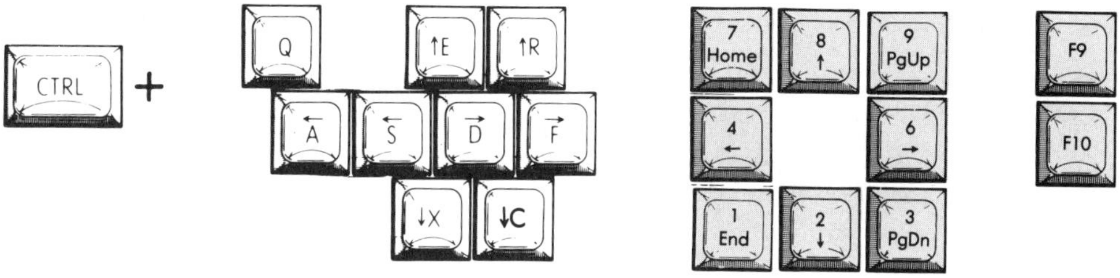

How They Are Used

Moving the Cursor UP:

[8 ↑] [CTRL] [E] One line.

[9 PgUp] [CTRL] [R] One screen.

[F9] [CTRL] [Q] [R] To start of file.

[7 Home] To top left of screen.

Moving the Cursor LEFT:

[4 ←] [CTRL] [S] One character.

[CTRL] [A] One word.

[CTRL] [Q] [S] To start of line.

Moving the Cursor RIGHT:

[6 →] [CTRL] [D] One character.

[CTRL] [F] One word.

[CTRL] [Q] [D] To end of line.

Moving the Cursor DOWN:

[2 ↓] [CTRL] [X] One line.

[3 PgDn] [CTRL] [C] One screen.

[F10] [CTRL] [Q] [C] To end of file.

[1 End] [CTRL] [Q] [X] To bottom of screen.

Quick Cursor Movement

Moving the Cursor to a Specified Place

CTRL Q F	To any character, word, or phrase you specify.
CTRL Q 0-9	To any place that has been marked with a numbered place marker (<0> to <9>).
CTRL Q B	To the beginning of a marked block.
CTRL Q K	To the end of a marked block.
CTRL Q P	To the cursor position before the last command. (Especially useful after ^KS command.)
CTRL Q V	To the cursor position before last find or replace command. OR: to the place where the last block was copied, moved or deleted *from* (i.e., the source of the block).

Scrolling the Text

The Keys Used

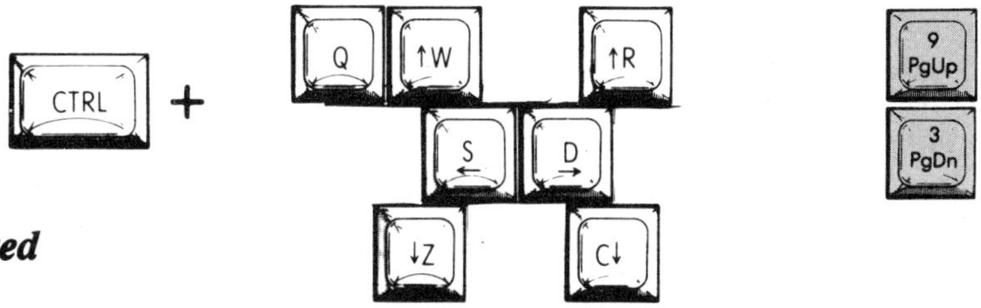

How They Are Used

Moving toward the TOP (beginning) of the file:
(Scrolling the Text DOWN)

CTRL W — One line.

9 PgUp — CTRL R — One screenful.

CTRL Q W — Continuously, line by line.

CTRL Q Q R — Continuously, screen by screen.

Moving toward the LEFT:
(Scrolling the Text RIGHT)

CTRL Q S

To beginning of line.

Moving toward the RIGHT:
(Scrolling the Text LEFT)

CTRL Q D

To end of current screen line.

Moving toward the BOTTOM (end) of the file:
(Scrolling the Text UP)

CTRL Z — One line.

3 PgDn — CTRL C — One screenful.

CTRL Q Z — Continuously, line by line.

CTRL Q Q C — Continuously, screen by screen.

Deleting Text

Deleting to the LEFT:

Del or CTRL ← (Use CTRL BACKSPACE when in NumLock).
One character.

CTRL Q ←
To start of line.

Deleting to the RIGHT:

CTRL G One character.

CTRL T To end of word.

CTRL Q Y To end of line.

Deleting both LEFT and RIGHT:

CTRL Y Entire line. *(to beginning and end)*

Deleting Specified Text:

CTRL K Y Delete a marked block.

CTRL Q A **Find?** *any text you want deleted.* Delete specified text.

Replace with? ↵

(See options in next section on "Searching and Replacing")

Searching and Replacing: Q uick Editing

Command:	*Function:*
CTRL Q F	Find specified character, word, or phrase (maximum 30 characters).
CTRL Q A	Find specified character, word, or phrase (maximum 30 characters) and Replace with specified character, word, or phrase (maximum 30).
CTRL L	Repeat last Find or Replace command.
CTRL Q V	Move cursor to last Find or Replace. OR: to cursor position before Find or Replace command.

Options:	*Function:*
n (any number from 1 to 65,535)	With ^QF: Find the nth occurrence. With ^QA: Find and Replace the next n occurrences.
B	Search backwards.
G	Global replace. Starting at beginning of file, search and replace through entire file. (Use with ^QA only.)
N	Replace without asking for OK.
U	Ignore upper- and lowercase when searching.
W	Search for whole words only.

Quick Editing (continued)

Searching for Marked Text:

Command:	*Function:*
CTRL Q 0-9	Find numbered placemarker (<0> to <9>). (See next section: "Marking Places and Blocks.")
CTRL Q B	Find the beginning of a marked block.
CTRL Q K	Find the end of a marked block. (See next section: "Marking Places and Handling Blocks.")

Marking Places and Handling Blocks

Placemarkers

Command:	*Function:*
CTRL K 0-9	Insert a numbered placemarker (<0> to <9>).
CTRL K 0-9	Hide or move a numbered placemarker.
CTRL Q 0-9	Find a numbered placemarker.

Marking Blocks

Command:	*Function:*
F7 CTRL K B	Mark the beginning of a block (<B>).
F8 CTRL K K	Mark the end of a block (<K>).

Finding Blocks

Command:	*Function:*
CTRL Q B	Find the beginning of block (<B>).
CTRL Q K	Find the end of block (<K>).
CTRL Q V	Find the previous position of block that was copied, moved, or deleted.

Handling Blocks

CTRL K H	Hide a marked block.
CTRL K C	Copy a marked block.
CTRL K W	Write (copy) a marked block to a separate file.
CTRL K V	Move a marked block.
CTRL K Y	Delete a marked block.

Handling Files

Command from the Opening Menu:	*from the Main Menu:*	*Function*
D		Edit a "document" file.
N		Edit a "non-document" file.
L	CTRL K L	Change a logged disk.
F	CTRL K F	List files on logged disk.
E	CTRL K E	Rename a file.
O	CTRL K O	Copy a file.
Y	CTRL K J	Delete a file.
	CTRL K W	Write (copy) block to separate file.
	CTRL K R	Read (copy) whole file into text.

Saving Files

Command:	*Function:*
CTRL K S	Resume. (Save file with latest changes and return to file. Use ^QP to return to where you were before you saved.)
CTRL K D	Done. (Save file with latest changes and return to opening menu.)
CTRL K X	Exit. (Save file with latest changes and return to operating system.)

Abandoning Files

Command:	*Function:*
CTRL K Q	Quit. (Abandon file and/or changes and return to opening menu.)

Miscellaneous Editing Commands

Command:	*Function:*
↵	End paragraph (with hard carriage return).
CTRL N	Insert hard carriage return.
⭾ or CTRL I	Tab. (Inserts tab in Insert Mode. Moves cursor to tab in Writeover Mode.)
0 Ins CTRL V	Turn insertion mode ON/OFF.
CTRL U . . . Esc	Interrupt last command typed.
CTRL Q Q	Repeat next command typed.

Formatting O n-Screen

Formatting Controls:

Command:	*Function:*	*Defaults* Document Mode:		*Defaults* Non-Document Mode:
F3 / CTRL O L	Set left margin.	column 1		column 1
F4 / CTRL O R	Set right margin.	col. 65 col. 60	(80-col.scrn) (64-col.scrn)	col. 65 col. 60
CTRL O X	Release margins.	n/a		n/a
CTRL O I	Set variable tab.	columns: 6, 11, . . ., 56		columns: 9, 17, . . ., 73
CTRL O N	Clear variable tab(s).	n/a		n/a
F2 / CTRL O G	Set temporary left margins at tab stop.	n/a		n/a
CTRL O F	Set margins & tabs according to ruler-line that cursor is on.	n/a		n/a
CTRL O S	Set line spacing.	1 (single spacing)		1
CTRL O C	Center line cursor is on.	n/a		n/a

Formatting Toggles:

Command:	*Feature Turned ON/OFF:*	*Defaults* Document Mode:	*Non-Document Mode:*
CTRL O E	Soft Hyphen Entry [ON: all hyphens typed will be soft]	OFF	OFF
CTRL O H	Hyphen Help [ON: prompts you to hyphenate (with soft hyphens) during ^B reform]	ON	OFF
CTRL O J	Justification [ON: inserts soft spaces to justify right margin]	ON	OFF
CTRL O W	Word-Wrap [ON: inserts soft carriage returns when you reach right margin]	ON	OFF
CTRL O V	Variable Tabs [ON: tabs as on ruler line; OFF: tabs every 8 spaces]	ON	OFF
CTRL O D	Display of Control Characters	ON	ON
CTRL O P	Display of Page-Breaks	ON	Inoperative
CTRL O T	Display of Ruler Line	ON	OFF

Special Printing Effects

***Printing Toggles:** (use in pairs)*

Command:	*Special Effect turned ON/OFF*	*How they appear on the screen:*	*How they appear on paper:*
F6 CTRL P B	Boldface	^Bboldface ^B	**boldface**
CTRL P D	Doublestrike	^Ddoublestrike ^D	**doublestrike**
F5 CTRL P S	Underscore	^Sunder score ^S	under score
CTRL P T	Superscript	superscript ^T1 ^T	superscript^{1}
CTRL P V	Subscript	subscript ^V1 ^V	subscript$_{1}$
CTRL P X	Strike-out	^Xstrike-out ^X	~~strike-out~~
CTRL P Y	Different ribbon color	change to ^Yred ^Y	change to red (*"red" appears in red*)

Printing Commands:

Command:	*Special Effect:*	*How it appears on screen:*	*How it appears on paper:*
CTRL P O	Non-break space	World ^OWar ^OI	World War I
CTRL P H	Overprint next character	Rene ^H´	René
CTRL P ↵	Overprint next line	_______________ underscore spaces	<u>underscore spaces</u>
CTRL P C	Stop print	^C	(printer stops)
CTRL P A	Alternate pitch	^A	(printer switches to alternate pitch)
CTRL P N	Standard pitch	^N	(printer returns to normal pitch)
CTRL P F	Print character assigned to "Phantom Space"	^PF	£ or ¢
CTRL P G	Print character assigned to "Phantom Rubout"	^PG	≠ or = or ⌉

Dot Commands: Controlling the Printer

Each dot command is entered on a separate line with the period in the first column.

	Command:	Function:	Default:	Units:	Default Equals:
Vertical Spacing and Layout	.LH	Line Height	8	1/48 inch	6 lines per inch
	.PL	Page Length	66	lines	11 inches
	.MT	Margin at Top	3	lines	1/2 inch
	.MB	Margin at Bottom	8	lines	1 1/3 inch
	.SR	Sub-Superscript "Roll"	3	1/48 inch	3/48 inch
Horizontal Spacing and Layout	.CW	Character Width	12	1/120 inch	10 chars. per inch (standard pitch)
			10	1/120 inch	12 chars. per inch (alternate pitch)
	.PO	Page Offset (from left of print-head starting position)	8	columns	4/5 inch
	.UJ	Microjustify	ON	1 = ON 0 = OFF	ON (add fractions of space between letters letters and words to justify right margin)
Pagination	.PA	Page-Break	n/a	n/a	n/a
	.CP	Conditional Page-Break	none	lines	n/a
	.PN	Page Number (for printout)	1	page number	start numbering pages with "1"
	.PC	Page Number Column	1/2 right margin	columns	middle column of page
	.OP	Omit Page Number	n/a	n/a	n/a
Headers and Footers	.HE	Header		n/a	no header (blank line)
	.FO	Footer		n/a	page # at column number set by .PC
	.HM	Header Margin (placement within top margin)	2	lines	1/3 inch from first line of text
	.FM	Footer Margin (placement within bottom margin)	2	lines	1/3 inch from last line of text
Miscellaneous	.BP	Bidirectional Print	1	1 = ON 0 = OFF	ON (prints left-to-right then right-to-left)
	.IG	Comment follows (does not print)	n/a	n/a	n/a
		Comment follows (does not print)	n/a	n/a	n/a

Getting On-Screen Help

Command:	*Function:*
F1 CTRL J H	Display and set the help level (0 to 3). 0 = the least amount of help and the most amount of space on the screen for text. 3 = the most amount of help and the least amount of space on the screen for text.
	Getting Help On:
CTRL J B	Paragraph Reforming (^B)
CTRL J D	Dot Commands
CTRL J F	Flags (in rightmost column of screen)
CTRL J I	Basic Editing
CTRL J P	Place Markers
CTRL J M	Margins and Tabs
CTRL J R	Ruler line
CTRL J S	Status Line
CTRL J V	Moving Text

IBM Function Keys

PC function key	*WordStar Function*	*Equivalent WordStar Command*
F1	Set help level	^JH
F2	Indent paragraph to tab	^OG
F3	Set left margin at cursor position	^OL ESC
F4	Set right margin at cursor position	^OR ESC
F5	Underline*	^PS
F6	Boldface*	^PB
F7	Mark beginning of block	^KB
F8	Mark end of block	^KK
F9	Move cursor to beginning of file	^QR
F10	Move cursor to end of file	^QC

* Put cursor at beginning and end of text you want underlined or boldfaced, then hit F5 or F6.

IBM Numeric Keypad

The operation of the numeric keypad (at the right end of the keyboard) is controlled by the Num Lock toggle. To enter numbers, press the Num Lock key. To use the edit functions, press the Num Loc key again.

Numeric Key	*WordStar Function*	*Equivalent WordStar Command*
4 ←	Move cursor left	^S
6 →	Move cursor right	^D
8 ↑	Move cursor up	^E
2 ↓	Move cursor down	^X
7 Home	Move cursor to top left of screen	^QE then ^QS
9 PgUp	Display previous screen (scroll down)	^R
3 PgDn	Display next screen (scroll up)	^C
1 End	Move cursor to bottom of screen	^QX
0 Ins	Insert	^V
. Del	Delete	DEL

Edit functions on numeric keypad will not operate with "Ctrl" key depressed.

Appendix B Summary of MailMerge™ Commands

Basic Definitions

Variable: Any piece of information that may change from one letter or document to another.

Example:

the *name* of the person you send a form letter to

Variable Name: Any name you make up to represent a variable.

Format Reminders:

- First character must be a letter.
- Other characters may be letters (uppercase or lowercase), numbers, or hyphens.
- No spaces or symbols other than hyphens are allowed.
- Minimum length is 1 letter.
- Maximum length is 40 characters.
- Each variable name must appear in the matrix document in a .RV, .AV, or .SV line (so MailMerge will know where to find the value for the variable).

Examples:

FirstName	*but not*	First Name	(*no spaces allowed*)
first-name	*but not*	1st-name	(*must start with a letter*)
Name-1	*but not*	Name#1	(*no symbols except hyphens*)

Variable Reference: A variable reference is the variable name enclosed in ampersands (&). It marks the place(s) in a letter or document where a variable will be inserted.

Format Reminders:

- ✓ Place ampersands before and after variable name.
- ✓ Spaces may be inserted between &s and variable name to improve readability.
- ✓ A variable reference may be followed by "/O" (slash/letter O) so that if the variable has no value, and if it is the only thing on a line, the line will be omitted. If there is no street address, for example, it will prevent a blank line between the name and the city/state on a mailing label.

Examples:

```
&FirstName&    or  &  FirstName  &
&first-name&   or  &  first-name  &
&Name-1&/O     or  &  Name-1  &/O
```

Variable Value: The piece of information that gets substituted for a variable reference in a letter or document. Values must come from a data file (via a .DF command) or from the operator (via .AV or .SV commands).

Format Reminders:

- ✓ Minimum length is zero characters (null value).
- ✓ Maximum length is 200 characters.

Example:

```
variable name       =  FirstName
variable reference  =  &FirstName&
variable value      =  John
```

Data File: A list of records containing variable values. Each record contains one set of variable values. Each variable value is one field or piece of information. Data files are usually name and address lists in which one record is one name and address (i.e., one set of information about a person or company).

Format Reminders:

- Records must be separated by carriage returns.
- Fields (variable values) must be separated by commas. (Spaces may be inserted around separator commas.)
- Enclose the field in quotes if a comma is part of the value.
- There must be the same number of fields in each record.
- If a field has no value, put a comma in its place.

Example Record:

Donna,Scanlon,"Sybex, Inc.",2344 Sixth St.,Berkeley,CA,94710

Example Field:

Donna (variable value for the variable FirstName)

Matrix File: The file you create that contains the text that stays the same from one printout to the next.

Format Reminders:

- Show where the variable values can be found, by means of .RV, .AV, or .SV command lines.
- Give the name of the data file (if one is used) in a .DF command line.
- Show where the variables will be inserted, by means of variable references embedded in the text.

Conditional Command: A dot command beginning with .IF or .EX that tells MailMerge under what conditions it should include a piece of text in the printout.

Example:

```
.IF &state& = "New York" GOTO
```

Format Reminders:

- Enclose the variable name in & (ampersand) symbols.

- Enclose the variable value in quotation marks.
- Leave a space between each item in the command (although a space before and after the = sign is optional).
- Enter a corresponding .EF (end) command for each .IF or .EX command.
- Conditional commands may not be more than 100 characters in length.
- There is no limit to the number of conditional commands.

End Command: A dot command beginning with .EF that marks the end of a section of text preceded by a conditional command.

Format Reminders:

- When a matrix document has more than one conditional command, .EF should be followed by a "label" identical to a label after GOTO in the corresponding conditional command.

Complex Conditional Command: A conditional command which specifies more than one condition. Conditions are joined by .AND. or .OR. .

Example:

```
.IF &amount& > "50" .AND. &amount& < "100" GOTO
```

Format Reminders:

- There must be a period before and after AND and OR.
- AND and OR must be in uppercase.
- Several conditions can be joined, but the command may not exceed 100 characters.

Label: A string of fewer than 20 characters that follows GOTO in a conditional command and .EF in the corresponding end command. When a matrix document includes more than one conditional command, the label lets MailMerge know how the conditional commands and end commands are paired.

Format Reminders:

- ✓ Never begin a label with a number, and never include spaces. (Use hyphens instead).

Example:

```
.IF &zip& = "10027" GOTO PARAGRAPH-3
(text . . .)
.EF PARAGRAPH-3
```

Comparison Characters: Symbols used in conditional commands to describe the variable value. There are eight comparison characters (see table in Chapter 12).

MailMerge Dot Commands

.DF *Data File.* Gives the name of the data file where MailMerge can find the values for variables.

Format Reminders:

- ✓ Follow .DF with the name of the data file.
- ✓ Include with the filename the drive where the file can be found—if not the logged drive.
- ✓ Add the word "CHANGE" to the .DF line if you want MailMerge to wait for you to change disks.
- ✓ A .DF line must be accompanied with a .RV command line.

Example:

```
.DF b:mainmail.lst CHANGE
```

.RV *Read Variable Values.* Tells MailMerge which variables are listed in the data file and in what order they appear.

Format Reminders:

- ✓ Follow .RV with the names of variables found in data file.
- ✓ The order and number of variable names must match the order and number of fields (values) in the data file.

- Variable names must be separated by commas and may be separated by spaces.

Example:

.RV FIRSTNAME, LASTNAME, COMPANY, STREET, CITY, STATE, ZIP

corresponding record in data file:

Donna, Scanlon, 2344 Sixth St., Berkeley, CA, 94710

.AV *Ask for Variable Value.* Tells MailMerge to ask the operator for a variable value.

Format Reminders:

- You may follow .AV with a message to the operator telling which value to supply and how to type it in. (Otherwise, the variable name will be the prompt.)
- Enclose prompt message in quotes and follow it with a comma.
- Follow .AV (or the "prompt") with the variable name.
- A comma and a number indicating the maximum length for the variable may follow the variable name (e.g., 2 for state abbreviations).

Example:

.AV "Type in the 2 letter code for state: ", STATE, 2

.SV *Set Variable Value.* Tells MailMerge what the value for a variable is. (See MicroPro's reference manual for more details.)

Format Reminders:

- Follow .SV with variable name.
- Follow variable name with a comma and then the variable value.

Example:

.SV DATE, February 20, 1985

.FI *Insert File.* Tells MailMerge where to insert another file when printing a file.

Format Reminders:

- ✔ Put .FI line at place in file where you want the other file inserted.
- ✔ Follow .FI with the name of the file to be inserted.
- ✔ Include disk drive if file is not on logged disk.
- ✔ Follow filename with the word CHANGE (for change disk) if file is in neither drive.

Example:

```
.FI b:chapt2b.txt CHANGE
```

.DM *Display Message.* Tells MailMerge to display a message on the screen while processing a document. Can be used to give information or help to the operator.

Example:

```
.DM Printing letter to &NAME&.
```

.CS *Clear Screen.* Clear the screen of any previous messages, and display new message (optional). Can be used to keep the screen uncluttered.

Example:

```
.CS
```

or

```
.CS Insert stationery for the next letter.
```

.IF "If . . ." Begins a conditional printing command. Tells MailMerge to omit the following section of text if the condition is met. Has the opposite effect from .EX.

Example:

```
.IF &amount& < "500" GOTO
```

Format Reminders (See *Conditional Command* under *Basic Definitions.*)

.EX "Except when . . ." Begins a conditional printing command. Tells MailMerge to omit the following section of text except when the condition is true. Has the opposite effect from .IF .

Example

```
.EX &amount& < "500" GOTO
```

Format Reminders (See *Conditional Command* under *Basic Definitions.*)

.EF "End of optional text" Marks the end of a section of text which is preceded by a conditional printing command. .EF can stand alone, but is often followed by a "label" indentical to a label at the end of the corresponding conditional command.

Appendix C Summary of SpellStar™ Commands

Getting Started

Menu:	*Command:*	*Function:*
Opening Menu	S	Run *SpellStar.* Bring up Operations Menu.
Operations Menu	C	*Check* a file for spelling errors. Bring up Spelling Check Menu.
	M	*Maintain* (update or create new) dictionaries. Bring up Dictionary Maintenance Menu.
	X	*Exit* SpellStar. Go back to Opening Menu.

Looking for Spelling Errors

Menu:	*Command:*	*Function:*
Operations Menu	C	*Check* a file. Bring up Spelling Check Menu.
Spelling Check Menu	D	Change the *dictionary.* (Name the main dictionary you want to use.) [Default = A:SPELSTAR.DCT]
	S	Add or change a *supplemental* dictionary. (Name the second dictionary you want to use—in addition to the main dictionary.) [Default = no supplemental dictionary]
	F	Change the *file.* (Name the file you want proofed.) [Default = file name entered under Opening Menu]
	W	Change the *work space.* (Name the disk (drive A:, B:) to put temporary work files on. Specify whichever one has free space.) [Default = logged disk]
	X	*Exit* Spelling Check Menu. Go back to Operations Menu.
	↵	*Proceed:* start checking the file for spelling errors.
(after SpellStar is done checking file)	L	*List* the misspelled words on the screen.
	R	Abandon the check and *return* to Operations Menu. *(The errors won't be flagged.)*

	↵	*Proceed:* mark the errors in the file with flags. flag = ^@ copy of file with flags = type .@@@
(after SpellStar is done flagging errors)	R	*Return* to Operations Menu. (Use if you don't want to correct the errors now.)
	↵	*Proceed:* go to file to search for flagged errors. Bring up Correction Menu.

Correcting Errors

Menu:	*Command:*	*Function:*
Correction Menu	F	*Fix* word. Brings up the main editing menu so you can correct flagged word.
	I	*Ignore* flag. (Use if word should not be changed.)
	B	*Bypass* word. (Allows you to come back to it later.)
	^L	Go to next flagged word.
	D	Add word to main *dictionary.* (SpellStar will create a separate word file, of type .ADD, with words to be added to a dictionary.)
	S	Add word to *supplemental* dictionary. (Word will be entered in .ADD file and flagged with an "S".)
	^QL	*Restart* search for flagged words. (Use this command to go back to bypassed words.) ↵ = search forward from cursor. G = search forward from beginning of file. B = search backward from end of file.
	^KD	*Save* corrected file. Go back to Opening Menu.

Creating and Revising Dictionaries

Menu:	*Command:*	*Function:*
Operations Menu	M	Bring up Dictionary *Maintenance* Menu.
Maintenance Menu	F	Change the word *file,* i.e., the file of words to be added to the dictionary (Usually, a .ADD file.) [Default = file name entered at Opening Menu]

	D	Change the *dictionary* to be updated. (Don't use if you want to *create* a new dictionary.) [Default = A:SPELSTAR.DCT]
	U	Change the name of *update* dictionary. Use to give a name to a new dictionary (if creating one) or to give a new name to the revised dictionary (if updating one).
	W	Change the *work space.* (Name the disk to be used for work space.) [Default = logged disk]
Toggle Options (YES/NO)	N	Create a *new* dictionary. [Default = NO]
	A	*Add* all the words in the word file to the dictionary. [Default = NO]
	T	*Delete* all the words in the word file from the dictionary you're revising. [Default = NO]
	C	*Combine* operations. Add *and* delete words. Add to the dictionary the words in the word file that are not in the dictionary. Delete from the dictionary the words that are in both files. [Default = YES]
	S	Create or revise a dictionary by using only the words in an .ADD word file that have been marked with an "S" (for *supplemental* dictionary). [Default = NO]
	L	*List* the dictionary on the screen. (Enables you to view the dictionary before changing it.) [Default = NO]
	↵	*Proceed:* begin creating or revising the dictionary according to the options selected above.

Appendix D Map of WordStar

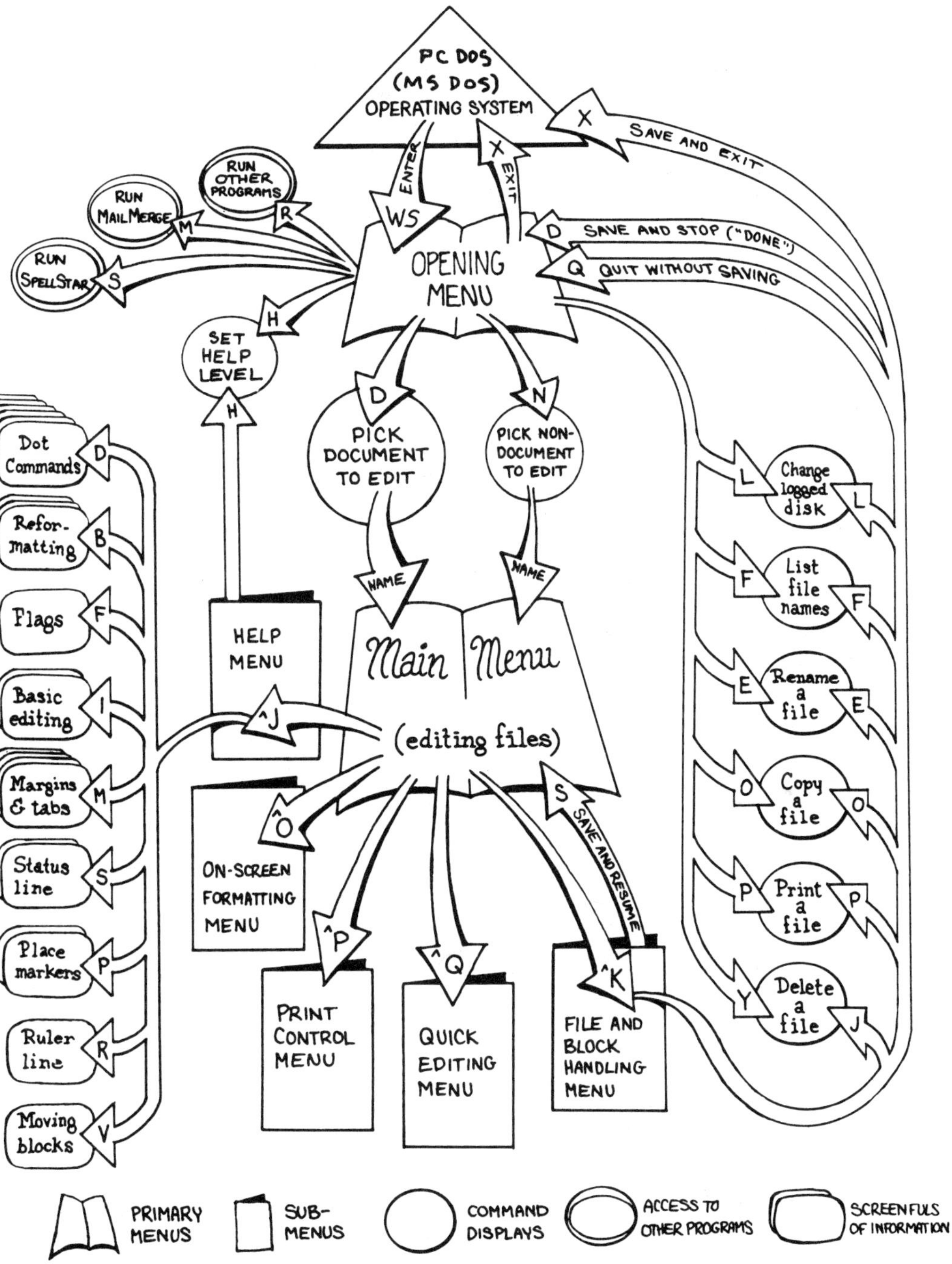
PC DOS
(MS DOS)
OPERATING SYSTEM
ENTER
WS
X
EXIT
X
SAVE AND EXIT
D
SAVE AND STOP ("DONE")
Q
QUIT WITHOUT SAVING
RUN OTHER PROGRAMS
R
RUN MAILMERGE
M
RUN SPELLSTAR
S
OPENING MENU
H
SET HELP LEVEL
H
D
PICK DOCUMENT TO EDIT
N
PICK NON-DOCUMENT TO EDIT
NAME
NAME
Main Menu
(editing files)
HELP MENU
^J
Dot Commands
D
Refor-matting
B
Flags
F
Basic editing
I
Margins & tabs
M
Status line
S
Place markers
P
Ruler line
R
Moving blocks
V
^O
ON-SCREEN FORMATTING MENU
^P
PRINT CONTROL MENU
^Q
QUICK EDITING MENU
S
SAVE AND RESUME
^K
FILE AND BLOCK HANDLING MENU
L
Change logged disk
L
F
List file names
F
E
Rename a file
E
O
Copy a file
O
P
Print a file
P
Y
Delete a file
J
PRIMARY MENUS
SUB-MENUS
COMMAND DISPLAYS
ACCESS TO OTHER PROGRAMS
SCREENFULS OF INFORMATION

Appendix E A Special Note about Earlier Versions of WordStar

In Chapter 8, I describe disk full problems that may occur when you're saving long files. If you're working with a version of WordStar earlier than 3.3, you might also encounter DISK FULL messages when you're moving backwards (particularly if you do it repeatedly). The reason is that WordStar must make a temporary copy of part of the file whenever you move the cursor any appreciable distance toward the start of the file. If the file is large, there may not be room on the disk for this temporary file, in which case you'll get a message that reads:

```
*** ERROR E 12: DISK FULL *** Press ESCAPE Key
```

After hitting Esc, you can recover by moving the cursor forward (that is, to the end of the file) with ^QC. Then save it with ^KS. Then you can move *forward* through the file to the place you were trying to move backward to. (If your disk is full enough, you can even run into problems moving forward.)

There are several things you should avoid doing to make sure disk full problems don't come up when you're moving around in a file.

1. Don't ^QR (move the cursor to beginning of the file) when you're far from the beginning of a long file.
2. Don't ^QW (scroll down) or continuously ^E (cursor up a line) in a long file.
3. Don't ^QP (cursor to previous position) or ^QV (cursor to position of last find or to source of moved block) when the previous position or source is a long way back.
4. Don't ^Q1, ^Q2, etc. (cursor to numbered marker) when the marker is a long way back.
5. Don't ^QB (cursor to block beginning) at the start of a large block in a large file.

In all these cases, use ^KS (save and continue to edit) to put the cursor at the beginning of the file.

There are two other times when you may encounter DISK FULL messages. The first is when you're using the block commands ^KW, ^KV, and ^KC in long files. The reason is that to carry out these commands, WordStar must move backwards through the file which—as I've already mentioned—involves making temporary copies of parts of the file on the disk.

You may also encounter DISK FULL messages when you're doing a global search and replace (^QA with the G option).

In a long file, if the cursor isn't near the beginning, ^KS before giving a global command with the G option. Otherwise, when the G option moves the cursor to the start of the file, it may produce a disk-full error. It's also a good idea to ^KS before ^QVing if the cursor isn't near the beginning.

However, ^KW uses less space on the disk than ^KV or ^KC. When you're moving a block of text a long distance, ^KW may work even when ^KV and ^KC give you trouble. You can substitute it for them in the following way:

^KW the block you want to move to a file called TEMP (or whatever). If you're moving the block to a point later on in the file, ^QZ down to that point. If you're moving it to an earlier point, save the file with ^KS to get the cursor to the beginning of the file, and then ^QZ down to the new location.

Once you get to the new location for the block, insert TEMP into the file with the ^KR command. Then kill TEMP with ^KJ. (You don't want your disk cluttered with temporary files that have served their purpose.) This procedure may seem like a lot of trouble, but it's a lot faster than your cursor creeping through a long file, and a lot easier than trying to recover from a disk-full error.

If, despite these precautions, you still get a DISK FULL message when you're using global search and replace commands, making block moves, or moving backwards in a long file, consult the section on Recovering from Full Disk Problems in Chapter 8.

Command and Symbol Index

Boldfaced page numbers indicate where the index entry is boldfaced in the chapters, and therefore, where it's most fully explained.

SpellStar Commands

Subject Index

POWER UP! KIDS' GUIDE TO THE COMMODORE 64™
by Marty DeJonghe and Caroline Earhart
192 pp., illustr., Ref. 0-188
Colorful illustrations and a friendly robot highlight this guide to the Commodore 64 for kids 8–11.

Humor

COMPUTER CRAZY
by Daniel Le Noury
100 pp., illustr., Ref. 0-173
No matter how you feel about computers, these cartoons will have you laughing about them.

MOTHER GOOSE YOUR COMPUTER: A GROWNUP'S GARDEN OF SILICON SATIRE
by Paul Panish and Anna Belle Panish, illustrated by Terry Small
96 pp., illustr., Ref. 0-198
This richly illustrated hardcover book uses parodies of familiar Mother Goose rhymes to satirize the world of high technology.

CONFESSIONS OF AN INFOMANIAC
by Elizabeth M. Ferrarini
215 pp., Ref. 0-186
This is one woman's tongue-in-cheek revelations of her pursuit of men, money, and machines. Learn about the many shopping services, information banks, and electronic dating bulletin boards available by computer.

Special Interest

COMPUTER POWER FOR YOUR LAW OFFICE
by Daniel Remer
142 pp., Ref. 0-109
How to use computers to reach peak productivity in your law office, simply and inexpensively.

THE COLLEGE STUDENT'S PERSONAL COMPUTER HANDBOOK
by Bryan Pfaffenberger
210 pp., illustr., Ref. 0-170
This friendly guide will aid students in selecting a computer system for college study, managing information in a college course, and writing research papers.

CELESTIAL BASIC
by Eric Burgess
300 pp., 65 illustr., Ref. 0-087
A collection of BASIC programs that rapidly complete the chores of typical astronomical computations. It's like having a planetarium in your own home! Displays apparent movement of stars, planets and meteor showers.

COMPUTER POWER FOR YOUR ACCOUNTING FIRM
by James Morgan, C.P.A.
250 pp., illustr., Ref. 0-164
This book is a convenient source of information about computerizing your accounting office, with an emphasis on hardware and software options.

PERSONAL COMPUTERS AND SPECIAL NEEDS
by Frank G. Bowe
175 pp., illustr., Ref. 0-193
Learn how people are overcoming problems with hearing, vision, mobility, and learning, through the use of computer technology.

ESPIONAGE IN THE SILICON VALLEY
by John D. Halamka
200 pp., illustr., Ref. 0-225
Discover the behind-the-scenes stories of famous high-tech spy cases you've seen in the headlines.

ASTROLOGY ON YOUR PERSONAL COMPUTER
by Hank Friedman
225 pp., illustr., Ref. 0-226
An invaluable aid for astrologers who want to streamline their calculation and data management chores with the right combination of hardware and software.

CP/M Systems

THE CP/M® HANDBOOK

by Rodnay Zaks

320 pp., 100 illustr., Ref 0-048

An indispensable reference and guide to CP/M—the most widely-used operating system for small computers.

MASTERING CP/M®

by Alan R. Miller

398 pp., illustr., Ref. 0-068

For advanced CP/M users or systems programmers who want maximum use of the CP/M operating system . . . takes up where our *CP/M Handbook* leaves off.

THE BEST OF CP/M® SOFTWARE

by John D. Halamka

250 pp., Ref. 0-100

This book reviews tried-and-tested, commercially available software for your CP/M system.

THE CP/M PLUS™ HANDBOOK

by Alan R. Miller

250 pp., illustr., Ref. 0-158

This guide is easy for beginners to understand, yet contains valuable information for advanced users of CP/M Plus (Version 3).

IBM PC and Compatibles

THE ABC'S OF THE IBM® PC

by Joan Lasselle and Carol Ramsay

143 pp., illustr., Ref. 0-102

This book will take you through the first crucial steps in learning to use the IBM PC.

THE BEST OF IBM® PC SOFTWARE

by Stanley R. Trost

351 pp., Ref. 0-104

Separates the wheat from the chaff in the world of IBM PC software. Tells you what to expect from the best available IBM PC programs.

THE IBM® PC-DOS HANDBOOK

by Richard Allen King

296 pp., Ref. 0-103

Explains the PC disk operating system. Get the most out of your PC by adapting its capabilities to your specific needs.

BUSINESS GRAPHICS FOR THE IBM® PC

by Nelson Ford

259 pp., illustr., Ref. 0-124

Ready-to-run programs for creating line graphs, multiple bar graphs, pie charts, and more. An ideal way to use your PC's business capabilities!

THE IBM® PC CONNECTION

by James W. Coffron

264 pp., illustr., Ref. 0-127

Teaches elementary interfacing and BASIC programming of the IBM PC for connection to external devices and household appliances.

BASIC EXERCISES FOR THE IBM® PERSONAL COMPUTER

by J.P. Lamoitier

252 pp., 90 illustr., Ref. 0-088

Teaches IBM BASIC through actual practice, using graduated exercises drawn from everyday applications.

USEFUL BASIC PROGRAMS FOR THE IBM® PC

by Stanley R. Trost

144 pp., illustr., Ref. 0-111

This collection of programs takes full advantage of the interactive capabilities of your IBM Personal Computer. Financial calculations, investment analysis, record keeping, and math practice—made easier on your IBM PC.

YOUR FIRST IBM® PC PROGRAM

by Rodnay Zaks

182 pp., illustr., Ref. 0-171

This well-illustrated book makes programming easy for children and adults.

DATA FILE PROGRAMMING ON YOUR IBM® PC

by Alan Simpson

219 pp., illustr., Ref. 0-146

This book provides instructions and examples for managing data files in BASIC. Programming design and development are extensively discussed.

SELECTING THE RIGHT DATA BASE SOFTWARE FOR THE IBM® PC

SELECTING THE RIGHT WORD PROCESSING SOFTWARE FOR THE IBM® PC

SELECTING THE RIGHT SPREADSHEET SOFTWARE FOR THE IBM® PC

by Kathleen McHugh and Veronica Corchado

100 pp., illustr., Ref. 0-174, 0-177, 0-178

This series on selecting the right business software offers the busy professional concise, informative reviews of the best available software packages.

THE MS™-DOS HANDBOOK

by Richard Allen King

320 pp., illustr., Ref. 0-185

The differences between the various versions and manufacturer's implementations of MS-DOS are covered in a clear, straightforward manner. Tables, maps, and numerous examples make this the most complete book on MS-DOS available.

ESSENTIAL PC-DOS

by Myril and Susan Shaw

300 pp., illustr., Ref. 0-176

Whether you work with the IBM PC, XT, PC*jr*, or the portable PC, this book will be invaluable both for learning PC-DOS and for later reference.

Software Specific

Spreadsheets

VISICALC® FOR SCIENCE AND ENGINEERING

by Stanley R. Trost and Charles Pomernacki

203 pp., illustr., Ref. 0-096

More than 50 programs for solving technical problems in science and engineering. Applications range from math and statistics to electrical and electronic engineering.

DOING BUSINESS WITH MULTIPLAN™

by Richard Allen King and Stanley R. Trost

250 pp., illustr., Ref. 0-148

This book will show you how using Multiplan can be nearly as easy as learning to use a pocket calculator. It presents a collection of templates for business applications.

MASTERING VISICALC®

by Douglas Hergert

217 pp., 140 illustr., Ref. 0-090

Explains how to use the VisiCalc "electronic spreadsheet" functions and provides examples of each. Makes using this powerful program simple.

DOING BUSINESS WITH VISICALC®

by Stanley R. Trost

260 pp., illustr., Ref. 0-086

Presents accounting and management planning applications—from financial statements to master budgets; from pricing models to investment strategies.

DOING BUSINESS WITH SUPERCALC™

by Stanley R. Trost

248 pp., illustr., Ref. 0-095

Presents accounting and management planning applications—from financial statements to master budgets; from pricing models to investment strategies.

MULTIPLAN™ ON THE COMMODORE 64™

by Richard Allen King

260 pp., illustr., Ref. 0-231

This clear, straighforward guide will give you a firm grasp on Multiplan's functions, as well as provide a collection of useful template programs.

Word Processing

INTRODUCTION TO WORDSTAR®

by Arthur Naiman

202 pp., 30 illustr., Ref. 0-134

Makes it easy to learn WordStar, a powerful word processing program for personal computers.

PRACTICAL WORDSTAR® USES

by Julie Anne Arca

303 pp., illustr., Ref. 0-107

Pick your most time-consuming office tasks and this book will show you how to streamline them with WordStar.

THE COMPLETE GUIDE TO MULTIMATE™

by Carol Holcomb Dreger

250 pp., illustr., Ref. 0-229

A concise introduction to the many practical applications of this powerful word processing program.

THE THINKTANK™ BOOK

by Jonathan Kamin

200 pp., illustr., Ref. 0-224

Learn how the ThinkTank program can help you organize your thoughts, plans, and activities.

Data Base Management Systems

UNDERSTANDING dBASE III™

by Alan Simpson

250 pp., illustr., Ref. 0-267

For experienced dBASE II programmers, data base and program design are covered in detail; with many examples and illustrations.

UNDERSTANDING dBASE II™

by Alan Simpson

260 pp., illustr., Ref. 0-147

Learn programming techniques for mailing label systems, bookkeeping, and data management, as well as ways to interface dBASE II with other software systems.

ADVANCED TECHNIQUES in dBASE II™

by Alan Simpson

250 pp., illustr., Ref. 0-228

If you are an experienced dBASE II programmer and would like to begin customizing your own programs, this book is for you. It is a well-structured tutorial that offers programming techniques applicable to a wide variety of situations. Data base and program design are covered in detail, and the many examples and illustrations clarify the text.

Integrated Software

MASTERING SYMPHONY™

by Douglas Cobb

763 pp., illustr., Ref. 0-244

This bestselling book provides all the information you will need to put Symphony to work for you right away. Packed with practical models for the business user.

SYMPHONY™ ENCORE: PROGRAM NOTES

by Dick Andersen

325 pp., illustr., Ref. 0-247

Organized as a reference tool, this book gives shortcuts for using Symphony commands and functions, with troubleshooting advice.

JAZZ ON THE MACINTOSH™

by Joseph Caggiano and Michael McCarthy

400 pp., illustr., Ref. 0-265

The complete tutorial on the ins and outs of the season's hottest software, with tips on integrating its functions into efficient business projects.

MASTERING FRAMEWORK™

by Doug Hergert

450 pp., illustr., Ref. 0-248

This tutorial guides the beginning user through all the functions and features of this integrated software package, geared to the business environment.

ADVANCED TECHNIQUES IN FRAMEWORK™

by Alan Simpson

250 pp., illustr., Ref. 0-267

In order to begin customizing your own models with Framework, you'll need a thorough knowledge of Fred programming languages, and this book provides this information in a complete, well-organized form.

ADVANCED BUSINESS MODELS WITH 1-2-3™

by Stanley R. Trost

250 pp., illustr., Ref. 0-159

If you are a business professional using the 1-2-3 software package, you will find the spreadsheet and graphics models provided in this book easy to use "as is" in everyday business situations.

THE ABC'S OF 1-2-3™

by Chris Gilbert and Laurie Williams

225 pp., illustr., Ref. 0-168

For those new to the LOTUS 1-2-3 program, this book offers step-by-step instructions in mastering its spreadsheet, data base, and graphing capabilities.

MASTERING APPLEWORKS™

by Elna Tymes

250 pp., illustr., Ref. 0-240

Here is a business-oriented introduction to AppleWorks, the new integrated software package from Apple. No experience with computers is assumed.

Languages

BASIC

YOUR FIRST BASIC PROGRAM

by Rodnay Zaks

182 pp., illustr. in color, Ref. 0-092

A "how-to-program" book for the first time computer user, aged 8 to 88.

FIFTY BASIC EXERCISES

by J. P. Lamoitier

232 pp., 90 illustr., Ref. 0-056

Teaches BASIC through actual practice, using graduated exercises drawn from everyday applications. Programs written in Microsoft BASIC.

BASIC FOR BUSINESS

by Douglas Hergert

224 pp., 15 illustr., Ref. 0-080

A logically organized, no-nonsense introduction to BASIC programming for business applications. Includes many fully-explained accounting programs, and shows you how to write your own.

EXECUTIVE PLANNING WITH BASIC

by X. T. Bui

196 pp., 19 illustr., Ref. 0-083

An important collection of business management decision models in BASIC, including inventory management (EOQ), critical path analysis and PERT, financial ratio analysis, portfolio management, and much more.

BASIC PROGRAMS FOR SCIENTISTS AND ENGINEERS

by Alan R. Miller

318 pp., 120 illustr., Ref. 0-073

This book from the "Programs for Scientists and Engineers" series provides a library of problem-solving programs while developing the reader's proficiency in BASIC.

Pascal

INTRODUCTION TO PASCAL (Including UCSD Pascal™)

by Rodnay Zaks

420 pp., 130 illustr., Ref. 0-066

A step-by-step introduction for anyone who wants to learn the Pascal language. Describes UCSD and Standard Pascals. No technical background is assumed.

THE PASCAL HANDBOOK

by Jacques Tiberghien

486 pp., 270 illustr., Ref. 0-053

A dictionary of the Pascal language, defining every reserved word, operator, procedure, and function found in all major versions of Pascal.

APPLE® PASCAL GAMES

by Douglas Hergert and Joseph T. Kalash

372 pp., 40 illustr., Ref. 0-074

A collection of the most popular computer games in Pascal, challenging the reader not only to play but to investigate how games are implemented on the computer.

PASCAL PROGRAMS FOR SCIENTISTS AND ENGINEERS

by Alan R. Miller

374 pp., 120 illustr., Ref. 0-058

A comprehensive collection of frequently used algorithms for scientific and technical applications, programmed in Pascal. Includes programs for curve-fitting, integrals, statistical techniques, and more.

DOING BUSINESS WITH PASCAL

by Richard Hergert and Douglas Hergert

371 pp., illustr., Ref. 0-091

Practical tips for using Pascal programming in business. Covers design considerations, language extensions, and applications examples.

Other Languages

FORTRAN PROGRAMS FOR SCIENTISTS AND ENGINEERS

by Alan R. Miller

280 pp., 120 illustr., Ref. 0-082

This book from the "Programs for Scientists and Engineers" series provides a library of problem-solving programs while developing the reader's proficiency in FORTRAN.

A MICROPROGRAMMED APL IMPLEMENTATION

by Rodnay Zaks

350 pp., Ref. 0-005

An expert-level text presenting the complete conceptual analysis and design of an APL interpreter, and actual listing of the microcode.

UNDERSTANDING C

by Bruce H. Hunter

320 pp., Ref 0-123

Explains how to program in powerful C language for a variety of applications. Some programming experience assumed.

FIFTY PASCAL PROGRAMS

by Bruce H. Hunter

338 pp., illustr., Ref. 0-110

More than just a collection of useful programs! Structured programming techniques are emphasized and concepts such as data type creation and array manipulation are clearly illustrated.

Technical

Assembly Language

PROGRAMMING THE 6502

by Rodnay Zaks

386 pp., 160 illustr., Ref. 0-135

Assembly language programming for the 6502, from basic concepts to advanced data structures.

6502 APPLICATIONS

by Rodnay Zaks

278 pp., 200 illustr., Ref. 0-015

Real-life application techniques: the input/output book for the 6502.

ADVANCED 6502 PROGRAMMING

by Rodnay Zaks

292 pp., 140 illustr., Ref. 0-089

Third in the 6502 series. Teaches more advanced programming techniques, using games as a framework for learning.

PROGRAMMING THE Z80®

by Rodnay Zaks

624 pp., 200 illustr., Ref. 0-069

A complete course in programming the Z80 microprocessor and a thorough introduction to assembly language.

Z80® APPLICATIONS

by James W. Coffron

288 pp., illustr., Ref. 0-094

Covers techniques and applications for using peripheral devices with a Z80 based system.

PROGRAMMING THE 6809

by Rodnay Zaks and William Labiak

362 pp., 150 illustr., Ref. 0-078

This book explains how to program the 6809 microprocessor in assembly language. No prior programming knowledge required.

PROGRAMMING THE Z8000®

by Richard Mateosian

298 pp., 124 illustr., Ref. 0-032

How to program the Z8000 16-bit microprocessor. Includes a description of the architecture and function of the Z8000 and its family of support chips.

PROGRAMMING THE 8086™/8088™

by James W. Coffron

300 pp., illustr., Ref. 0-120

This book explains how to program the 8086 and 8088 microprocessors in assembly language. No prior programming knowledge required.

PROGRAMMING THE 68000™

by Steve Williams

250 pp., illustr., Ref. 0-133

This book introduces you to microprocessor operation, writing application programs, and the basics of I/O programming. Especially helpful for owners of the Apple Macintosh or Lisa.

Hardware

FROM CHIPS TO SYSTEMS: AN INTRODUCTION TO MICROPROCESSORS

by Rodnay Zaks

552 pp., 400 illustr., Ref. 0-063

A simple and comprehensive introduction to microprocessors from both a hardware and software standpoint: what they are, how they operate, how to assemble them into a complete system.

MICROPROCESSOR INTERFACING TECHNIQUES

by Rodnay Zaks and Austin Lesea

456 pp., 400 illustr., Ref. 0-029

Complete hardware and software interfacing techniques, including D to A conversion, peripherals, bus standards and troubleshooting.

THE RS-232 SOLUTION

by Joe Campbell

194 pp., illustr., Ref. 0-140

Finally, a book that will show you how to correctly interface your computer to any RS-232-C peripheral.

MASTERING SERIAL COMMUNICATIONS

by Joe Campbell

250 pp., illustr., Ref. 0-180

This sequel to ***The RS-232 Solution*** guides the reader to mastery of more complex interfacing techniques.

Operating Systems

SYSTEMS PROGRAMMING IN C

by David Smith

275 pp., illustr., Ref. 0-266

This intermediate text is written for the person who wants to get beyond the basics of C and capture its great efficiencies in space and time.

THE PROGRAMMER'S GUIDE TO UNIX SYSTEM V

by Chuck Hickev/Tim Levin

300 pp., illustr., Re.f 0-268

This book is a guide to all steps involved in setting up a typical programming task in a UNIX systems environment.

REAL WORLD UNIX™

by John D. Halamka

209 pp., Ref. 0-093

This book is written for the beginning and intermediate UNIX user in a practical, straightforward manner, with specific instructions given for many business applications.

INTRODUCTION TO THE UCSD p-SYSTEM™

by Charles W. Grant and Jon Butah

300 pp., 10 illustr., Ref. 0-061

A simple, clear introduction to the UCSD Pascal Operating System for beginners through experienced programmers.

Computer Specific

Apple II—Macintosh

THE PRO-DOS HANDBOOK

by Timothy Rice/Karen Rice

225 pp., illustr., Ref. 0-230

All Pro-DOS users, from beginning to advanced, will find this book packed with vital information. The book covers the basics, and then addresses itself to the Apple II user who needs to interface with Pro-DOS when programming in BASIC. Learn how Pro-DOS uses memory, and how it handles text files, binary files, graphics, and sound. Includes a chapter on machine language programming.

THE MACINTOSH™ TOOLBOX

by Huxham, Burnard, and Takatsuka

300 pp., illustr., Ref. 0-249

This tutorial on the advanced features of the Macintosh toolbox is an ideal companion to The Macintosh BASIC Handbook.

THE MACINTOSH™ BASIC HANDBOOK

by Thomas Blackadar/Jonathan Kamin

800 pp., illustr., Ref. 0-257

This desk-side reference book for the Macintosh programmer covers the BASIC statements and toolbox commands, organized like a dictionary.

PROGRAMMING THE MACINTOSH™ IN ASSEMBLY LANGUAGE

by Steve Williams

400 pp., illustr., Ref. 0-263

Information, examples, and guidelines for programming the 68000 microprocessor are given, including details of its entire instruction set.

THE EASY GUIDE TO YOUR APPLE II®

by Joseph Kascmer

147 pp., illustr., Ref. 0-122

A friendly introduction to the Apple II, II plus, and the IIe.

BASIC EXERCISES FOR THE APPLE®

by J.P. Lamoitier

250 pp., 90 illustr., Ref. 0-084

Teaches Applesoft BASIC through actual practice, using graduated exercises drawn from everyday applications.

THE APPLE II® BASIC HANDBOOK

by Douglas Hergert

250 pp., illustr., Ref. 0-115

A complete listing with descriptions and instructive examples of each of the Apple II BASIC keywords and functions. A handy reference guide, organized like a dictionary.

APPLE II® BASIC PROGRAMS IN MINUTES

by Stanley R. Trost

150 pp., illustr., Ref. 0-121

A collection of ready-to-run programs for financial calculations, investment analysis, record keeping, and many more home and office applications. These programs can be entered on your Apple II plus or IIe in minutes!

YOUR FIRST APPLE II® PROGRAM

by Rodnay Zaks

182 pp., illustr., Ref. 0-136

This fully illustrated, easy-to-use introduction to Applesoft BASIC programming will have the reader programming in a matter of hours.

THE APPLE® CONNECTION

by James W. Coffron

264 pp., 120 illustr., Ref. 0-085

Teaches elementary interfacing and BASIC programming of the Apple for connection to external devices and household appliances.

THE APPLE IIc™: A PRACTICAL GUIDE

by Thomas Blackadar

175 pp., illustr., Ref. 0-241

Learn all you need to know about the Apple IIc! This jargon-free companion gives you a guided tour of Apple's new machine.

THE BEST OF EDUCATIONAL SOFTWARE FOR APPLE II® COMPUTERS

by Gary G. Bitter, Ph.D. and Kay Gore

300 pp., Ref. 0-206

Here is a handy guide for parents and an invaluable reference for educators who must make decisions about software purchases.

YOUR SECOND APPLE II® PROGRAM

by Gary Lippman

250 pp., illustr., Ref. 0-208

The many colorful illustrations in this book make it a delight for children and fun for adults who are mastering programming on any of the Apple II line of computers, including the new IIc.

THE MACINTOSH™: A PRACTICAL GUIDE

by Joseph Caggiano

280 pp., illustr., Ref. 0-216

This easy-to-read guide takes you all the way from set-up to more advanced activities such as using Macwrite, Macpaint, and Multiplan.

MACINTOSH™ FOR COLLEGE STUDENTS

by Bryan Pfaffenberger

250 pp., illustr., Ref. 0-227

Find out how to give yourself an edge in the race to get papers in on time and prepare for exams. This book covers everything you need to know about how to use the Macintosh for college study.

Atari

YOUR FIRST ATARI® PROGRAM

by Rodnay Zaks

182 pp., illustr., Ref. 0-130

This fully illustrated, easy-to-use introduction to ATARI BASIC programming will have the reader programming in a matter of hours.

BASIC EXERCISES FOR THE ATARI®

by J.P. Lamoitier

251 pp., illustr., Ref. 0-101

Teaches ATARI BASIC through actual practice, using graduated exercises drawn from everyday applications.

THE EASY GUIDE TO YOUR ATARI® 600XL/800XL

by Thomas Blackadar

175 pp., illustr., Ref. 0-125

This jargon-free companion will help you get started on the right foot with your new 600XL or 800XL ATARI computer.

Introducing SYBEX Elf . . .

. . . a new standard in communications software

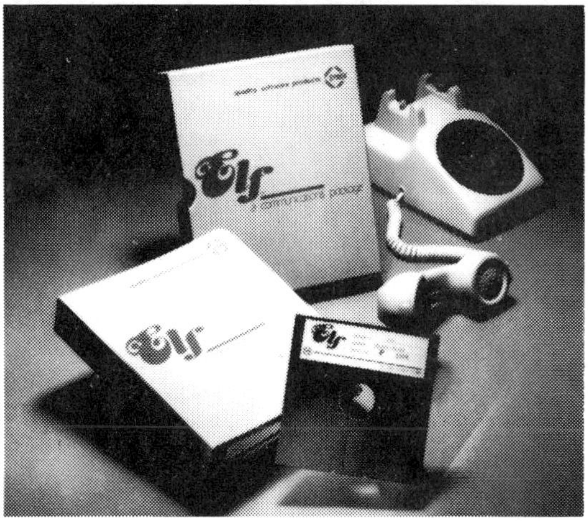

Friendly and sophisticated, Elf provides automated access to virtually any computer, unlimited-size file transfer, and compatibility with every conceivable operating system.

- Menu driven
- Easily customized
- Crash-proof error handling
- Password-protected host mode
- Supports XMODEM protocol
- Superb SYBEX documentation

IBM PC version only $125; for CP/M, $85

Call SYBEX today for full details! (800) 227-2346

HALF-PRICE BOOK OFFER!

Complete and return the form below to order your copy of Elf, and get the new SYBEX data-sharing reference book for only $11.48—50% off the regular price!

Data Sharing with 1-2-3 and Symphony, Including Mainframe Links, by Dick Andersen. Solutions to all your data-sharing problems, including discussions of dBASE II and III, Framework, Multiplan; downloading and uploading with mainframes. Thirteen authoritative chapters with a quick-reference index.

☐ Send me more details on state-of-the-art communications with SYBEX Elf.

☐ Yes, I'll take advantage of your half-price book offer—include my copy of *Data Sharing with 1-2-3 and Symphony* for only $11.48 with my copy of Elf.

☐ Send my copy of Elf today!

☐ IBM PC version—$125 ☐ CP/M version—$85

Name ______________________________

Address ______________________________

City, state, ZIP ______________________________

☐ Check enclosed

☐ Charge my:

☐ Visa ☐ MasterCard ☐ American Express

Credit card # ________________ exp. date __________

SYBEX Computer Books, 2344 Sixth Street, Berkeley, CA 94710

800-227-2346

SYBEX Computer Books are different.

Here is why . . .

At SYBEX, each book is designed with you in mind. Every manuscript is carefully selected and supervised by our editors, who are themselves computer experts. We publish the best authors, whose technical expertise is matched by an ability to write clearly and to communicate effectively. Programs are thoroughly tested for accuracy by our technical staff. Our computerized production department goes to great lengths to make sure that each book is well-designed.

In the pursuit of timeliness, SYBEX has achieved many publishing firsts. SYBEX was among the first to integrate personal computers used by authors and staff into the publishing process. SYBEX was the first to publish books on the CP/M operating system, microprocessor interfacing techniques, word processing, and many more topics.

Expertise in computers and dedication to the highest quality product have made SYBEX a world leader in computer book publishing. Translated into fourteen languages, SYBEX books have helped millions of people around the world to get the most from their computers. We hope we have helped you, too.

For a complete catalog of our publications: